How Far We Have Travelled

Travelled

The Voice of Mary Holland

Selected by Mary Maher

**TOWN
HOUSE**
DUBLIN

First published in 2004 by

TownHouse, Dublin
THCH Ltd
Trinity House
Charleston Road
Ranelagh
Dublin 6
Ireland

www.townhouse.ie

Author photograph © Jane Bown, The Observer

1 2 3 4 5 6 7 8 9 10

A CIP catalogue record for this book is available from the
British Library.

ISBN: 1-86059-241-4

Typeset by Typeform Ltd

Printed by Bookmarque Ltd, Croydon, Surrey

Contents

Introduction by Mary Maher   ix

1985
Why the Flynn case is so important   1
Hating Britain and loving her largesse   5
Putting the temptresses in their places   9

1986
A number one song at the National Stadium   13
An issue the Liverpool boat can't carry away   18
Why Sinn Féin should not be underestimated   22
AIDS: the "Irish solution" will not work   27

1987
What now of the causes and crusades?   32
Some facts of Irish life always with us   36
Making the red poppy a symbol of division   40

1988
Hume and Adams and historical resonances   44
Could any of us have shouted "Stop"?   48
A political necklacing for Haughey?   52
A remarkable resilience gives hope   56
Tax dodgers rush in from the cold   60

1989
Examining roots of Ulster loyalism   64
Some things did change in 20 years   68
A few days home may mark the change   73

1990
Virgin takes risks on safe sex   77
A "Dear John" letter from Mary   82
IRA brings anarchy one step nearer   87

1991
An emotional attachment to the UN   92
Wrong time to keep out Sinn Féin   97

1992

A woman's right to speak denied   101
Why a "Yes" vote can further the interests of Irish women   104
Disenfranchised resentful at exclusion from change   109
Afraid to be identified   113

1993

Bewilderment over society's failure to provide protection   117
Courage to back an unpopular cause may light the way ahead   121
Have they gone far enough for Sinn Féin to deliver the IRA?   126

1994

Families in failed marriages need understanding, not criticism   131
Loyalist violence yet to appear on agenda   136
Reminder of iniquity in State's extended "family"   140
Time has come to draw line under past   144

1995

Frightened women may get only fudge and a list   147
Did Dev save the soul or skin of Ireland?   152
Putting past behind to give peace a chance   157
AIDS scare may make us wary of warnings from altars   161
Tongues of fire as hope and history rhyme   165
Time has arrived to abolish the Irish solution   169
Politicians must forge working relations for peace   174

1996

Bus bombs may give republican doves room to move   179
Lectures on "welfare fraud" ring very hollow   183
Christmas wrapping cannot cover the hostility   187

1997

Irish in Britain are still suffering prejudice   192
Harryville gesture revives hopes for resolution   197
Attacks on media must not deter them from doing job   201

1998

After being driven mad with grief, long political slog resumes   205
Formula needed to surmount latest peace hurdle   209

1999

Sinn Féin must look at the figures that back a political way   213
Referendum essential to decide on Ireland's PfP role   217
Trimble has to convince party it has nothing to fear but fear   221
Old allies re-emerge to criticise women who go to work   225

2000

A gruesome memorial to a failure to shout "Stop"   229
Orangemen may lose all marching on   233

2001

The anger we must not ignore   237
Observer was willing to look at North   241

2002

Resignations set important precedent   245
Give thanks for how far we have travelled   249
What is the stars? That is the question   253

Introduction

Mary Holland was urged on numerous occasions to produce a book, a definitive summation of her work or a collection of her columns, or both. She always resisted. Despite the many prestigious awards accumulated over her lifetime, she never presented herself as other than a journeyman journalist: a reliable artisan, a wordsmith who reported and reflected on events as they happened, without an eye to permanence or posterity.

Knowing this, I approached the task of editing this collection of her columns from *The Irish Times* a little uneasily, wondering whether we were entitled to dispute her judgment.

My doubts dissolved rapidly. From the start, what emerged from these columns – some sixty, spanning three decades – was in stark contradiction of that maxim which holds that learning history from journalism is like telling time by the second hand on a clock.

It is like learning history as it happens. This is the best of what journalism can do, record the moment so vividly and perceptively – and often with such comic wit – that to read it is to re-live the moment. In the case of Mary Holland, it is also to find proof that now and then a journalist of rare ability places a handprint on history itself.

Both John Hume and Seamus Heaney have paid tribute to her unique role in the shaping of Northern Ireland's recent history. Only a fraction of that work is included here, but there is a wealth of material now available to students of journalism and politics. They will be astounded at how accurate she was in her assessments; how often she was vindicated; how very often she foreshadowed what was to come.

But much the same can be said of her columns on the

broader issues that faced the island of Ireland at the end of the twentieth century: human rights; social justice; the arts; church, state and power; the interplay of national and world politics. Hers was a voice that could not be ignored, marking every milestone and turning point. As Geraldine Kennedy, Editor of *The Irish Times*, said at her funeral: "She interfered with our comfort zones and challenged all of us."

I have a favourite column in this book. It was written in May 2002, shortly before Mary retired. It was at the time of the Roy Keane crisis, and we were in the same company when the inevitable row erupted over who was in the right. I had imagined Mary would support my position, which was anti-Keane, on a vaguely socialist principle that the greater good of the team was what mattered. She took a different view.

A week later she wrote: "...the memories which sustain my belief in the human spirit are not of the announcement that a deal had been struck on the terms of the Belfast Agreement, or of Margaret Thatcher and Garret FitzGerald signing the Anglo-Irish Treaty in 1985. They are of great performances by those whom we rightly call stars because they shed light upon our lives for years to come and in ways that we cannot fully comprehend...

"We common mortals owe a debt that we can never fully repay to those whom the gods have chosen as performing artists – actors, musicians, athletes. It is they who give us the stuff of dreams in our youth and memories in our declining years. We should value them accordingly."

I don't know that I agree with her yet. But I do know that a journalist who wrote as magnificently as she did also sustains our belief in the human spirit. This book is a gesture toward valuing her accordingly.

Mary Maher
October 2004

1985

Why the Flynn case is so important

MARCH 13, 1985

The Bishops have been sublimely discreet about Mr Justice Costello's decision to reject Eileen Flynn's appeal against unfair dismissal. So has Mrs Gemma Hussey, whose Department not only paid Miss Flynn's salary but also, on behalf of the taxpayer, contributes 80 per cent of the costs of running the convent school in which she has worked. As far as I can discover the views of the Department, which must have a heavy financial interest in the career of a teacher whom it paid to train, were not ascertained in any of the courts and tribunals which upheld the decision of the Holy Faith nuns to get rid of Miss Flynn.

For the Hierarchy, gathered this week at Maynooth, the decision in the Flynn case is a victory at least as important as their recent defeat on the Family Planning Bill. Even the bishops accept that the argument over contraception had been largely lost and that the recent dust-up was over where the lines get drawn, who gets to buy contraceptives legally and when.

Control over education is quite another matter and one in which the battle lines have not even been drawn. It is in the schools that children learn the values that turn them into

1

seriously committed members of Family Solidarity and SPUC. No one, certainly not the present government, is going to question the Irish Church's right to instill those values in children at the taxpayers' expense. It is even less likely to do so now that it has seen what happened to the 30-year-old schoolteacher who tried to question one small area of the Church's authority – its right to determine private, out-of-hours behaviour of its employees.

As I write, not one front-bench politic – whose uncle so roundly attacked the Church's attempts to interfere with his plans for secondary education – seems to think that the dismissal of this secondary school teacher has any long-term implications for the good health of the Republic.

The defeat of Miss Flynn must have been the sweeter because it was not necessary for a single bishop to raise his voice, in public at least, to achieve it. It has been left to the foot soldiers of the Church Militant to let the rest of us know just how important the Flynn case may yet prove to be.

Brother Declan Duffy, director of the Catholic Secondary School Secretariat, greeted last Friday's High Court judgment thus: "Without doubt a negative decision would have threatened the very existence of Catholic schools in this country."

To appreciate why a decision in favour of Miss Flynn could have had such apocalyptic repercussions from the Church's point of view, one needs only to look at the changing structure of the personnel employed in 521 secondary schools in the Republic, of which 443 are run by Catholic religious orders. Three hundred of these schools are run by nuns.

In recent years there has been a dramatic increase in the proportion of lay teachers employed in these schools compared to numbers of nuns and priests. Partly this is due to the increased numbers of teachers employed overall in secondary education, partly to the drop in religious vocations among men and women. Between 1970 and 1980 the proportion of religious teachers to lay teachers fell from 35 to 21 per cent. Today there are 11,990 teachers employed in secondary schools of whom 10,019 are lay and 1,881 members of religious orders.

In the same period teaching has lost something of its prestige as a profession with the usual inevitable result: more women go into teaching than men. At the moment 55 per cent of teachers are women and the vast majority of them are employed by the Church, even though their salaries are paid out of public funds. No wonder that it was a matter of crucial importance that Eileen Flynn should lose her case. In the wake of it, the rights of teachers in all Catholic schools – to be judged presumable by the quality of their teaching, to live their personal lives as they choose out of school hours – have been seriously weakened.

No one disputes that there were other issues that complicated the Flynn case, just as nobody seems seriously to question that she was a sensitive teacher with a rare ability to enthuse her students. Would she have had more support from politicians and from the media if she had not been a member of Sinn Féin? If there was civil divorce in this country and she had been able to marry the father of her child would she have been dismissed?

This was at the heart of the recent Canadian case which Declan Costello cited in which a Catholic teacher was fired because she married a divorced man in a civil ceremony. But in Vancouver the school system is public and non-denominational and parents who deliberately choose to send their children to a Catholic school must be presumed to be committed practising Catholics.

As important, a good teacher in a Canadian school who loses her job because of a disagreement of this nature with her employers will be able to find employment elsewhere, a luxury not easily available to Miss Flynn.

All these considerations pale into insignificance beside the principle at the heart of the case. In theory, the Irish Government controls education in this State. It certainly pays for it. For how much longer will it shell out huge sums of money to schools where it has no control over the quality of the teachers hired and fired, and where people are now more likely to be employed and promoted because they are good Catholics rather than for any talent they may have for educating children?

Much the same situation applies in the North where a succession of British ministers have had their fingers burnt trying to implement a policy which many of the people who live there would dearly like to happen: integrated education. But at least the British admit that they have other reasons for not squaring up to the bishops. A few years ago a British minister told me of his experience in trying to introduce some measure of desegregation in one area of education in the North. He met the local bishop for whom he had the highest regard, not least because the prelate in question was an implacable opponent of the IRA.

At their meeting the bishop intimated in the most civilised and diplomatic way, that if the minister was determined to press ahead with his interesting but wholly unacceptable ideas for integrated education he, for his part, might find it difficult to be quite so hard on the IRA in future. The plans were dropped. As Donogh O'Malley put it in the Senate in 1967 describing his problems with the bishops, "Christian charity, how are you?"

Hating Britain and loving her largesse

APRIL 10, 1985

They unveiled three new graves in the Republican plot in Derry cemetery, high over the River Foyle, on Easter Sunday afternoon. Each bore the familiar headstone, a grey Celtic Cross with the words "In proud and loving memory of Volunteer X who died for Ireland".

The purple silk stuff was removed from the headstone by two mothers and one young widow of the men who had died.

Many in the crowd who had come to mourn were middle-aged women, chain-smoking with old coats that were pulled too tightly about them. Most of the others were hardly more than boys and girls, scarcely out of their teens, too young to remember the Civil Rights movement or Bloody Sunday, or much of the recent history which took place in this lovely city and sparked off our present discontent.

It was a bleak enough ceremony. A biting wind blew in from the river so that the fine rain cut the faces and soaked through the inadequate clothing of the thousand or so people who had gathered outside the Bogside Inn to march to the cemetery.

None of the big names among the Provos was there to speak. An exotic note was struck by a small, very cold contingent, representing a group of Nicaraguan musicians who are currently touring Ireland. An interpreter said they had insisted on coming, despite the pressure from the Free State Government and from the SDLP that they should stay away.

Their leader gave us, in Spanish, a history of the Nicaraguan revolution stretching over 20 years, and the concentration of his audience was not helped by the rain becoming colder and more insistent.

A young woman read the 1916 Proclamation. A boy in a white shirt and black trousers shivered as he read a roll-call of honour of those from Derry who had died for Ireland during the present Troubles. The roll-call consisted of those who had volunteered to die for Ireland when they joined the Provisional IRA. No mention was made of the hundreds of others who made no such choice but died anyway.

The ritual seemed almost perfunctory, as though the Provisionals, in Derry at least, no longer need to put on the kind of performance and rhetoric which stirs the blood of its supporters.

There was only one moment which set the crowd alight and brought the British Army helicopter scurrying back to the scene, video-cameras at the ready.

That was when three men in green uniforms, wearing the statutory balaclavas, fired a volley of shots from the platform. A middle-aged woman turned to me and said: "Thank God, thank God they're still with us."

I asked one man, whose family had suffered terribly for its commitment to the Provisional IRA, whether he thought it had been worth it, the dead young men and women in Derry, and the 257 from Ireland as a whole whose names are given in this week's *An Phoblacht*.

He shook his head and said he didn't know any more. But no such doubts aggravated the young men and women who stayed to the end of the speeches, the rain soaking through their thin jeans and denim jackets.

Never has one been so conscious of the base the Provos have among the deprived, the young, the unemployed.

In Dublin these youngsters might turn to joyriding or petty crime. Here they stop, bless themselves in front of the graves of dead hunger strikers, faintly embarrassed that a stranger should see them in this act of piety.

I counted 19 Tricolours flying in the cemetery. What kind of Ireland do these youngsters dream of? What it is that attracts them in the Republic, that they should risk ending in one of these small grey graves?

A local priest said to me recently: "I'm not sure they think much about the South at all. You have to understand their whole experience has been of being stopped, searched and harassed by the security forces. They're not interested in any compromise; in fact, they probably think of Gerry Adams as middle-aged. They want a victory and that means not just the British soldiers gone but the RUC and UDR smashed."

Peter Barry has spoken eloquently of the responsibility of the Irish Government to end "the nightmare of the nationalist minority". Charley Haughey repeats that the only answer to the problem of the North lies in a unitary state for the country as a whole. It's almost impossible to imagine how the young people gathered in Derry cemetery last Sunday envisage a united Ireland.

They know very little about the Republic except that drink and almost everything else is a lot more expensive across the Border. Yet the pictures and graffiti which cover the walls on the Bogside speak of some yearning for an idealised sense of Irishness, grim determination not to be beaten back into defeat.

Yet almost everything that makes life bearable for Derry's poor, at least in the material sense, is due to the British

Welfare State. The social dereliction and decay in the streets immediately around the cemetery is grim, but the new estates which stretch out on the border of the city contain some of the most attractive housing in the British Isles. The cuts under the Thatcher Government have been extremely hard but, as always, Northern Ireland has been shielded from the worst savagery.

The centre of Derry is evidence of this special treatment. On Saturday afternoon the shops in the gleaming new Richmond Centre were crowded with people from the Creggan and Bogside buying Easter outfits for their children and food at prices to make any visitor from the South weak with envy.

Already I've been told about families who, some years ago when the violence was at its height, decided to move across the Border to the Republic. At that time the prospect of trying to rear children at Derry seemed too dangerous and difficult. Now these families are trying to sell the houses they bought in Donegal and move back to Derry.

They want a united Ireland but they also want lower taxes, cheaper consumer goods, a free medical service and the possibility of third-level education for their children. The Welfare State under Mother England still offers them those things.

It is an issue which is often overlooked when Peter Barry talks of the nightmare of the nationalist minority, real though that agony continues to be in many ways.

Charles Haughey never talks about it when he addresses the subject of British withdrawal and the need for a united Ireland. There could be another nightmare in the offing. What will happen to the nationalist minority if Britain tires of paying the bills which makes life bearable for many of them?

Putting the temptresses in their places

OCTOBER 9, 1985

The Kerry Babies Report is not moving as well as the original reviews seemed to promise. Of a print order of 1,800, only a fraction have been sold. In some ways this is a pity. The extracts published in the newspapers do not convey the banal inadequacy of a report which we had hoped would illuminate some of the darker reaches of our society. Mr Justice Lynch's report combines the sexual attitudes of James Hadley Chase with a style reminiscent of Jeffrey Farnol.

The main interest of his report is the portrait of the author as a certain type of Irishman and as a compendium of his views on women, the peasantry, and the need to defend the status quo.

Much attention has been given to the chapter entitled 'Public Attitudes' and to Mr Justice Lynch's outrage at the public displays of sympathy for Joanne Hayes, compared with the lack of bouquets, Mass cards and public assemblies for the wife of Jeremiah Locke. In fact, by far the greater part of this chapter is taken up with repeating a warning which Mr Lynch gave when the tribunal was sitting in Tralee.

He explained, in no uncertain terms, to members of the public and to the media the deference which he believed was properly due to the tribunal and to himself. "When a High Court judge comes to a country town, he is very often offered guards of honour and the like. I have shunned all of these," he announced, before going on to warn of what would happen if "even a silent and peaceful picket" appeared in the vicinity of the courthouse.

Not only would any protesters be sent to prison, but they could expect to spend a considerable time cooling their heels. "I rather think I would find it convenient to hear an application for release, so long as I continue to sit here in Tralee, whether that will be a period of three, four, five or six weeks."

With this admonition hanging over them, it is perhaps not surprising that members of the public at the time and journalists since have felt a bit wary of reminding Mr Justice Lynch why there were demonstrations in support of Joanne Hayes, why she was sent Mass cards, flowers and letters from all over the country. It was not because she had an affair with a married man, or even because she had a baby in pretty dreadful circumstances.

The protests and the sympathy were provoked by Mr Justice Lynch's conduct of the tribunal, the way in which he allowed the most prurient and brutal probing of Ms Hayes's sexual activities and of the physical details of her pregnancies.

Cross-examination of this kind has not disappeared from our courts but usually some kind of check is put on it. Cases involving family problems are held *in camera*, because we believe it is positively destructive for them to be heard in public. Even in rape cases, where it is often held necessary to question the woman harshly in order to protect the rights of the accused man, her name is not made public.

Mr Justice Lynch and members of his profession will argue that this tribunal was set up in response to widespread public concern about the methods employed by the gardaí, and that it was therefore essential for its hearings to be conducted in public.

Even so, many of us who attended, even briefly, those early days in Tralee, found it difficult to understand why Joanne Hayes had to be questioned in the way that she was. Why was it necessary to allow senior counsel so to harass her about the details of her private life that she could only continue giving evidence after sedation? The judge, we knew, had it in his discretion to protect her not only from certain lines of questioning, but from the tone adopted by some senior counsel.

Those of us who had attended the Stardust Tribunal recalled the care with which Mr Justice Ronan Keane had treated the teenage survivors of the tragedy, when barristers tried to push them too far about whether they had been drinking that night.

Now, reading the report, it is clear why the questioning was allowed to proceed in the way that it did. In Mr Justice Lynch's estimation, the wrongdoers – to borrow a word – in this story are the three women of the Hayes family.

Mrs Hayes, unrecognisable to anyone who saw her walking heavily to and from the court, is a cold, inflexible woman obsessed with defending her family "escutcheon". Kathleen is "very tough, intelligent and tenacious", a rural Lady Macbeth who makes the decisions for the family when the going gets tough. Joanne? Well, we all know about Joanne.

By comparison, the Hayes brothers are seen as more sinned against than sinning: Ned "a softer character than his two sisters", furiously fingering his rosary beads in court when the strain of sustaining a false story begins to tell; slow, suggestible Mike who responded well to "an appeal to the spiritual". (You think I'm exaggerating? Read the report for yourself.) As for the Garda Síochána – a bit "slipshod" in their methods, a little over-familiar and contemptuous of the oath, somewhat inclined to elevate "honest suspicions into positive fact", but nothing to compare with the perjury of Mrs Hayes, "lying through her teeth".

The women were to blame because women tempt men, conceive children, and make an unholy mess of things when nobody wants to be left holding the baby. On top of that these women had the temerity to complain about their betters who had made them sign statements confessing to crimes they had not committed.

This report reinforces attitudes which have been with us since the Book of Genesis: "It was the woman Thou gavest to be with me Lord. She gave me of the tree and I did eat."

1986

A number one song at the National Stadium

MAY 28, 1986

The conflicting – and angry – reactions of the Government parties to Mr Des O'Malley's speech at his party's conference constitute the most convincing evidence yet for the claim that the Progressive Democrats just might herald a breakthrough in Irish politics. They also demonstrate that, whatever the original reasons for its formation, the party is no longer just about Charlie Haughey.

It is Labour and Fine Gael which have been made most uncomfortable by what Mr O'Malley had to say to a rapt audience at the National Stadium on Saturday night. Mr Dick Spring finds his proposals for dramatic cuts in income tax and public spending "crazy and selfish", designed to steal from the very poor in order to subsidise the rich. Mr John Bruton thinks that the promise of such dramatic tax cuts could be damaging for democracy. By contract, Mr Peter Barry shares the PDs' ambition to bring the standard rate of income tax down to 25 per cent, though he questions their timescale for achieving it. Mrs Gemma Hussey is reported to be impressed by the "realism" of what Mr O'Malley had to say about social welfare policies, including, presumably, the desirability of cutting public spending in these areas.

For the moment Fianna Fáil is silent, content, as usual, to watch the Coalition parties quarrelling in public and exposing the deep political differences that still exist between them. Sooner or later, though, even Fianna Fáil is going to have to confront the challenge posed by Mr O'Malley's new party and the ideas it is putting before the Irish people. Specifically, it will have to consider whether Fianna Fáil (or anyone else) can hope to continue indefinitely gathering votes right across the social spectrum, if there is even one party prepared to offer a clear, unequivocal economic policy designed to appeal, powerfully, to the self-interest of one section of the electorate.

Whatever about the other TDs on the blue and orange platform last Saturday night, Mr O'Malley is now refreshingly explicit as to how he sees the role of the Progressive Democrats. He made no apology for concentrating almost exclusively on economic policy, still less for the new right direction in which he believes the economy should be steered. The PDs' solution to our chronic economic malaise lies in a drastic break with the consensus politics of the past decade or more. Mr O'Malley advocates cuts in income tax and public spending, an unapologetic "rolling back" of the State (on the grounds that the vast majority of Irish people have no sympathy for socialist ideas anyway), incentives for entrepreneurs, and welfare services geared only to the most needy in our society.

In case his audience missed the implications of all this, or chose to ignore it, Mr O'Malley hammered home his theme from the platform and in radio and television interviews. The Progressive Democrats are not to be a catch-all, populist party taking votes from all classes and conditions. Their appeal will be to the middle-class salary earner who sees his/her pay cheque disappear in tax, to the small businessman who finds it is impossibly difficult to expand his business and thus create new jobs, to the highly educated young who leave Ireland for job opportunities abroad.

If this sounds like the politics of naked self-interest, that isn't quite how Mr O'Malley himself sees it. There is a moral as well as an economic dimension to his political credo, and one which might prove powerfully attractive in a country which has embraced "Self Aid" as an appropriate response to the problems of mass unemployment. There is a gritty passion to Mr O'Malley's rhetoric when he speaks of the damage done to the fabric of society by the burgeoning black economy, the almost general endorsement of the view that it is socially acceptable to boast about not paying one's income tax or of cheating the State in other ways.

By contrast, the concern he evinces for those many thousands of people who remain deprived and disadvantaged sounds almost perfunctory. In a typewritten script that ran to 36 pages there were very few pages devoted to health, education, to possible improvements in our social services. Mr O'Malley did not begin to try to explain how his party would honour its pledge to care for the poor in a political climate where all the emphasis would be on cutting public spending. Even Mrs Thatcher now goes out of her way to try to convince the British electorate that the Welfare State is safe with her, though the weight of the evidence is that when you cut back to make the social services selective, the poor sink deeper and deeper into the trap of poverty.

Mr O'Malley would almost certainly argue that his priority at this conference was to spell out economic ideas to an audience, inside the National Stadium and way beyond it, which is very rarely asked to think in such terms. And, to be fair, his fierce determination not to equivocate did extend beyond the economy to take in the North and the divorce referendum. But it is on his economic policies that he has asked to be judged and here his message is so stark that it could well frighten off even those potential voters to whom it is designed to appeal.

Research in Britain has shown that even middle-class, middle-of-the-road voters who long for a reduction in income tax do not want this to be achieved at the cost of destroying the Welfare State. They fear the emergence of a society in which the poor are doomed to become poorer. Even in Britain, where class divisions and class politics are more overt, there appears to be little appetite for the creation of two nations. That is why Mrs Thatcher is under such pressure to present a more "caring" face to the electorate and to enter the run-up to the election with a more balanced team in government. In Ireland, where the folk memory of truly searing poverty is still quite recent, even middle-class voters are a lot less likely to approve of a party which is perceived to advocate swingeing attacks on the social services.

The Progressive Democrats need to demonstrate convincingly that they have a human heart as well as economic policies. There is a partial answer to the problem within their own ranks. For all its talk of breaking old moulds the party has decided to appoint a defector from Fine Gael as its deputy leader. The symbolism in terms of Irish politics is so banal as to be almost insulting to an electorate that is being urged by the PDs themselves to forget Civil War politics. No harm to Mr Michael Keating, but he does not have the presence, on or off the platform, to provide a much-needed balance to Mr O'Malley's impatient, intellectual image.

It is difficult to understand, even in electoral terms, why Ms Mary Harney was bypassed. To anyone who has attended any of the PDs' public meetings it is obvious that she is seen as the social conscience of the party. She sets an audience alight and makes them feel better for having listened to her, a literally invaluable asset in a politician. When the Progressive Democrats were first formed, it was easy to dismiss her speeches as full of heartwarming rhetoric but lacking any real political substance. That may well have changed, at least if one is to judge by her fine speech on Sunday winding up the debate on law reform.

Walking away from the National Stadium on Sunday, one was left with the impression of a group of people who are clever, professional, and a bit too keen on looking after Number One. Mary Harney can do quite a lot to counter that and to give the Progressive Democrats a caring face, but she cannot do it on her own. She needs to know, as do the voters, that her leader supports her.

An issue the Liverpool boat can't carry away

JUNE 25, 1986

On Monday night, after the Taoiseach had made his final campaign speech before the referendum, one of the speakers from the floor of the packed public meeting asked Dr FitzGerald if he did not feel profoundly depressed by the tenor of much of the debate. He cited the scare tactics, the talk of slippery slopes and opening floodgates, the evident lack of any trust in the maturity of the Irish people by some of those who oppose the introduction of divorce.

The Taoiseach said that, no, on the whole he didn't agree. We are a society in transition, moving from being very conservative, and in recent years we have been asked to come to terms with profound social changes very fast. What should cheer us up, Dr FitzGerald suggested, is that at least we can discuss the issues.

At times in recent days it has been depressing to see the posters and read the advertising designed to exploit the fears of those who feel most vulnerable in our society. "This amendment will impoverish women", "You could be divorced against your will", "Divorce is a child's nightmare" – these and others are aimed at women with children who are worried not just about property but about their place in the community generally. It tells us something desperately sad about the situation of women in Ireland today that such slogans should have had a major impact on the debate.

Against this, it should be stressed, and quite strongly, that the level of discussion at many public meetings, on the doorstep, in the media has been characterised by a social concern and moral tolerance which is quite different from the pro-life amendment campaign only three years ago. Monday's Fine Gael rally was an example of this. People came to it with all kinds of questions and views, some of which were passionately held and against the majority opinion in the audience, which was predominantly Fine Gael.

When the meeting was thrown open to the public, one man strode to the front of the hall, took the microphone, held aloft a copy of the Constitution and began to ask a long question about where compassion should be directed in a case where a father of six children was proposing to abandon them for a woman who herself had seven children.

He was fired with the insistent eloquence of the true believer who sees the television cameras within his grasp and kept coming back to the floor of the hall. In England, or in any other country I have known, he would have been thrown out when it became obvious that he could well wreck the whole evening. Instead he was treated with amazing tolerance, not just by Dr FitzGerald but by the general consensus in the audience, which ensured that he continued to get a hearing. Because he was not ejected as a martyr, robbed of the opportunity to make his case, he came to sound like a dotty fanatic and the meeting continued around him.

People got up and spoke with nervous eloquence of their own experience of unhappy marriages. One woman said how much it meant to her that the problem had at last been debated publicly and that some attempt had been made to deal with it. Even if the vote went against her on Thursday she would be grateful for that. Others questioned Dr FitzGerald on facilities in the new family courts, the impact on the North, pension rights, the Irish press, the details of the wording.

There was even rather a good joke about whether the Coalition would be filing for divorce now that the union was proved to have failed over five years. Most of the questions, though, were deeply serious and concerned about the social implications of the amendment.

There have been – and again we should recognise their importance – heroes and heroines in this campaign. These are people whom it has cost quite a lot in terms of their own religious convictions to come to terms with the need for this constitutional amendment. Most of us have known quite well from the day the referendum was announced which way we were going to vote. The issues are clear-cut and do not trouble our conscience one way or the other.

For some people the process has not been so easy. They are committed Catholics who, throughout their lives, have drawn strength and confidence from the teachings of the Church. Yet they have come to see that there is a public duty to deal with the problem of marriages that do break down and of extending to others the second chance which the Church denies. One thinks of a number of Fine Gael TDs and of priests and nuns who have insisted on expressing publicly their support for the amendment.

The case was put most eloquently at a meeting last week by Joe Doyle of Fine Gael, when he appealed for generosity from those who would never want a divorce towards those who have not been so lucky, because "life is difficult and stubborn and does not work out as people planned".

Mr Doyle made another point which is worth reiterating in the final days of the campaign. There are a lot of angry and unhappy people in Ireland who want a legal remedy in their own country for their marital problems. They want legal relationships recognised by society, and legitimate children. If the amendment is rejected, it will mean that their fellow countrymen have passed an adverse moral judgment on them, which is likely to make them very bitter.

These are some of the arguments one has heard in public halls and hotel meeting-rooms in recent weeks, and they do us some credit as a people. Sometimes it has seemed that the whole emphasis in the public debate has been on property rights, but there has been another side to it which has been more concerned with the kind of society we want in this country. We are not an ungenerous people, though we are often frightened and lack confidence about our own ability to cope with social change. It may be that tomorrow the caution and fear about the future will triumph and the amendment will after all be defeated.

That will be a setback, and a very serious one for many people, but it will not be the end of the story. The divorce issue will not go away and, unlike abortion, cannot be pushed out of sight on the Liverpool boat. This debate has been conducted in much less moralistic terms than other such arguments in the recent past. There has been widespread recognition that there is a problem of human suffering here with which Ireland is going to have to come to terms and not through a sterile debate about desirable moral absolutes. That in itself is an important step forward and will affect the way we look at this and other issues in the future.

Why Sinn Féin should not be underestimated

NOVEMBER 5, 1986

So, everyone from Garret FitzGerald through to Gerry Adams thinks that Sinn Féin can't win any seats, at least not in the next election. Don't believe it. The party leaders are worried, as they should be, and Gerry Adams, shrewd as ever, is hedging his bets.

The Provos learn from their mistakes. Politically, it is one of the qualities which makes them much more interesting to observe than most of the parties in the state. Once, just once, they threw caution to the winds and boasted about how well they would do in an election. That was when Danny Morrison stood against Hume for the EEC parliament and Sinn Féin predicted that he could win. Before, and ever since, they have been aggressively cautious in estimating their votes. This has meant that when they do well at all, we in the media fall over ourselves with amazement at the results.

It is in Sinn Féin's interests to keep saying that they can't possibly take a single seat in the next election. Its leaders have to think not only of the media and other political parties but, much more importantly, of their own members. They have just been through an extremely traumatic debate in which the

leadership overturned the whole weight of the historic arguments ranged against it.

The debate has caused great bitterness and may not be over
yet. Very many people, including some who went along
reluctantly with the change in policy, are waiting for Adams
and the others to be proved wrong. If they say that they are
hopeful of taking even one seat and then fail to do so, there
will be loud recriminations that they have sown bitterness and
confusion and misled the movement. If, on the other hand,
they do not win a seat, having protested that this was an
impossible task, how doubly sweet will be their victory.

When the political leaders opine that Sinn Féin cannot take
a seat they are fleshing out Gerry Adams' David and Goliath
scenario.

The votes for the Provos are not there at the moment but
nobody can say for certain that that will still be the case when
an election is called. A note of caution here. Do not trust,
entirely, what the opinion polls say about voting intentions in
relation to Sinn Féin. Over the years the polls in the North
have underestimated their vote because people are reluctant
to admit their support for a party which is so universally
reviled from the pulpit and in the media for its links with the
IRA. Something of the same caution almost certainly applies
here.

Examination of the Sinn Féin vote in the North also shows
that many people who have voted for the party do not
automatically support the IRA. But a vote for Sinn Féin is the
strongest possible protest which an alienated and deprived
section of the community can register at the ballot box. Does
anybody deny that such a vote exists down here. The question
is, can Sinn Féin mobilise it?

Politicians in the Republic will argue that there are objective
differences. It is true that there is no identifiable nationalist
community in which a lot of people are willing to support

Sinn Féin at the polls just to "show the Brits" what they think of the Government, the police and the courts. Even so, there are parts of inner-city Dublin where the similarities to the Falls and the Bogside are a lot more striking than the differences between them.

Apart from the hunger strike which started it all, the single factor crucial to Sinn Féin's electoral success in the North was the party's single-minded determination in mobilising the young and disaffected unemployed who, traditionally, do not vote in elections at all. They drew them into the party organisation and they got them to the polls. At last week's ard-fheis the rows upon rows of ardent young faces eloquently demonstrated just how far the party has gone along this road in the South. And they have hardly started yet.

But, it will be argued, people will not vote for a party which has links with the IRA. I wonder how much that will matter in the secrecy of the polling booth. For a start, the IRA does not operate a campaign down here. People do not have to worry about threats and intimidation and wonder whether it is right to shoot off-duty policemen. They know that the IRA is violent but then the whole of the North is violent and the IRA is only one part, our part, of the mess.

There is, too, a harsher reality. In some areas of Dublin, and perhaps of other large cities, the shadowy presence of the IRA in the background is no handicap at all to Sinn Féin. Rather the reverse. Ordinary decent people have to face, day after day, the dreadful problems that accompany poverty and social deprivation – chronic unemployment, debt, marital break-down, drugs, alcoholism. Many of these problems involve violence, threatened or real. Too often the police are unwilling or unable to help. So are the social service agencies. Only the Church provides some kind of support and that necessarily, is of a moral nature.

Here is a simple story of everyday life in one housing estate in north Dublin, in Mr Haughey's constituency as a matter of fact. An unmarried mother lives alone with her son. She complains of the noise made, night after night into the early hours, by her neighbours. She is threatened, quite violently, and so is her boy whom she is afraid to leave alone when she goes out to work. She goes to the police who say they can do nothing. The free legal advice people suggest that she take out a private prosecution. The local Fianna Fáil counsellor is sympathetic but can only direct her back to the police. She makes contact with Sinn Féin. Within 24 hours a member of the party comes to see her and listens to her story. He then goes to the troublesome neighbour and convenes a meeting between the two. There are no more threats. She does not think the Sinn Féin man mentioned the IRA. He didn't need to.

A much more dramatic example of the same phenomenon was the Concerned Parents against Drugs. Sinn Féin and the IRA were accused of "exploiting" the drugs issue for their own ends. What does any politician do, who takes up a local issue and campaigns on it? The sin here, presumably, was that the possible presence of the IRA persuaded drug pushers to move out of areas in a way that the police could not achieve. It is a condemnation which isn't likely to carry much weight with those parents who wanted their children protected from drugs.

And what of the North? We are told that people down here don't care about the North and that, insofar as they do think about it, they are deeply hostile. The Provos know this. It is one of the main reasons they want to become much more involved politically on this side of the Border. At their ard-fheis, several speakers in favour of dropping abstentionism made the point that they wanted to campaign on a platform that would be relevant and credible to voters in the Republic.

Adams and the others know that they cannot achieve their objectives in Northern Ireland without winning political support in the South. Already, by dropping abstentionism a whole range of issues, which were previously hovering on the margins, have arrived in the mainstream of political debate – Section 31, relations between Sinn Féin and other political parties, the effect this change of policy will have on the Provos themselves. And, as I said, they have only started.

AIDS:
The "Irish solution" will not work

DECEMBER 17, 1986

You found the abortion referendum depressing? You just hated the poll on divorce? Gentle reader, brace yourself. Very soon now those campaigns are going to seem like models of calm and rational debate as the country, belatedly, faces up to the necessity of dealing with AIDS.

Already, we have a foretaste of what is to come from the British experience. There, the Catholic bishops have joined forces with the Church of England to criticise the government's public education campaign because of the emphasis it places on "safe" sexual intercourse rather than a return to the Christian ideal of chastity.

The view of the moral majority was given vehement expression by James Anderton last week in a speech worthy of the right wing of Fine Gael. The Chief Constable of Greater Manchester spoke of sexual degenerates "swirling about in a human cesspit of their own making" and said that homosexuals should be asked why they engaged in "obnoxious sexual practices".

The response of the British government to this kind of thing has been robust. Norman Fowler, the Social Services Secretary, has said that its first priority must be to try and halt the spread of a virus which, he predicted, could kill between 500,000 and three million people in the next five years.

Faced with such a crisis, he said, no government could afford the luxury of a moral debate on sexual behaviour. It must accept the practical realities of the situation, one of which is the fact that young people's attitudes to sex are very different today from what they were 30 years ago.

Mr Fowler and his junior Ministers can afford to be resolute in public because the issue has already been fully debated within the Cabinet.

Some Ministers, including Mrs Thatcher, were extremely worried that a Conservative government committed to family life and Victorian values would be open to severe criticism if it launched a campaign which seemed to accept promiscuity as a fact of life, and concentrated on urging people to be more selective in their choice of sexual partner and to "play safe" when having sex by using a condom.

In the end, the practical pressures of the crisis dictated the explicit, non-judgmental tone of the campaign. But those who have been involved in devising the advertising have been well aware of the dangers of a formidable backlash, not only from the moral majority but from very many, ordinary, confused and anxious members of the general public.

One experienced commentator told me that a major factor which had enabled the government to adopt a calm, morally neutral line in its advertising was the fact that AIDS had now passed into the heterosexual community.

If it were still mainly confined to homosexuals and to drug users it would have been almost impossible to fight the popular view that AIDS is a gay plague, an act of retribution from a vengeful God who, even in pagan Britain, always seems that bit more credible when he is punishing people for their pleasures.

The advertising campaign may seem alarmingly frank over

here, but in Britian itself many doctors feel that it does not go half far enough. Some of those who advised the government wanted a much glossier hard sell, closer to the American advertisements which show young bodies intertwined and carry the message "Make it Safe".

How will we deal with the issue here? The latest figures from the Department of Health show that at least 13 cases of the disease have been notified and that eight of these have died. Just over 500 people have been found to have AIDS antibodies and the latest research from West Germany indicates that 80 per cent of these will probably go on to develop the disease itself.

For the moment most of the publicity has been about drug abusers, partly because the use of an infected needle means that the user risks injecting antibodies directly into the bloodstream, partly because drug-taking prisoners are the one major group of people at risk who have been effectively screened.

Already, given the extent of our drug problem, it is possible to see the kind of moral dilemma we are going to have to debate. Should we do as the Dutch have been doing and the British are just beginning to do: operate clinics where drug users can obtain sterile needles if they hand in used ones? Or will this be seen as condoning, even abetting the drug habit?

This, at least, is a fairly simple issue politically. But what this, or probably the next, Government is going to have to face is that in Ireland as everywhere else, AIDS is most likely to be spread by sexual intercourse.

Even in this country more people still have sex with more than one partner than take drugs. AIDS is no respecter of people's sexual preferences and, increasingly, it will affect the heterosexual community. The young – and we have the largest young population in Europe – will be particularly vulnerable because they have sex more often and with more partners.

There are two safeguards against the disease. One is chastity or a monogamous marriage in which both partners adhere to the ideal of total fidelity. The temptation for any Irish Government will be to bow to the all-too-predictable pressure from the Churches and their various support groups and base its public education campaign on the permissible joys of Christian marriage.

Fianna Fáil, whose leader is known to be against divorce, will presumably be particularly inclined towards this Irish solution to an Irish problem. Unfortunately it will not work.

Extolling the Christian view of sex will not stop AIDS any more than it has stopped unwanted pregnancies or marital breakdown. People will continue to have sex outside marriage and if their partner has AIDS they will risk contracting the antibodies.

Faced with such a threat, a responsible government will have to consider a campaign of public education which not only stresses the risks but also explains the practical safeguards that do exist against AIDS. By far the most important of these is the use of a prophylactic which reduces the risk of semen entering the bloodstream, i.e. a condom.

The British government, which has no theological problem with this issue, is still finding it very difficult to convince young, sexually active people. The young do not like condoms for a variety of reasons and have become accustomed to the availability of more acceptable methods of contraception.

To try and overcome this antipathy, considerable ingenuity is being devoted to getting condoms sold in those places where the young regularly shop – boutiques, record stores and so on. How on earth will our political leaders deal with all this?

The quality of the moral questions we are about to hear debated can probably be predicted from the abortion campaign. Is it all right to use a condom if it isn't being used for contraceptive purposes?

Is it more acceptable for homosexuals to use condoms (since they can't get pregnant anyway) or less? How will the Government target the gay community, given that homosexuality is still illegal?

Will any campaign explain that anal intercourse is particularly dangerous, again given that buggery is illegal under the 1861 Act even between heterosexual partners? What about oral sex? The debate has not even started yet. As I said, brace yourselves.

1987

What now of the causes and crusades?

FEBRUARY 4, 1987

D
o any of our political leaders think that Dominic McGlinchey should have been allowed, however briefly, to pay his last respects to his dead wife and to tell his children that they still have a father who cares about them? As I understand it, from listening to his brother-in-law talking to Pat Kenny, Mr McGlinchey's family did not request that he be allowed to attend his wife's funeral, or even the removal of the remains. What they asked for was that he might be given the opportunity, under any restrictions deemed necessary by the Garda, to see his wife's body and to calm his children who had seen their mother being shot dead.

What advice would those who are competing for our votes give to those Irish doctors who are currently much concerned about whether they will in future be able, legally, to talk to their women patients about abortion? We must presume from their silence that they do not consider that Mr Justice Hamilton's decision in the SPUC case has important implications which extend to anyone who wants to provide a full counselling service to pregnant women in distress.

Does Peter Barry believe that it makes sense to woo Rhonda Paisley onto RTÉ television to talk to her father, while forbidding the national broadcasting service from talking to the UDA, whose proposals for power-sharing in Northern Ireland constitute the most important initiative to come from the Unionist majority in the North since the signing of the Anglo-Irish Agreement? The Taoiseach must know that in this instance the effect of Section 31 has been that the UDA's overtures have sunk without trace down here, and we have had no opportunity to gauge how political parties in the Republic would respond to their proposals for a round-table conference on devolution.

The case against Section 31, as far as Sinn Féin is concerned, was argued most eloquently in this space yesterday by Declan Kiberd. Here's just one more point. If, as we keep being told, this election campaign is characterised by widespread public disillusion with all established politicians we can expect a very large protest vote. The obvious protest ticket is Progressive Democrat for the middle-class voter who has a job, Sinn Féin for the working-class unemployed.

The Provos themselves keep saying they won't win any seats, but as in the past they will take more votes than anyone expects. We should be able to see and hear them on television and radio.

I raise these questions, quite at random, to suggest that there ought to be other issues in this election besides the management of the economy. I understand very well, thank you, that unemployment is the most important thing on people's minds and that unless the economy is brought under some kind of rational control, the slide into social anarchy in this country could accelerate dangerously. Even so, there are other criteria which we should consider in assessing our politicians which may be just as important as the ability to juggle the budget deficit figure as a proportion of GNP.

There is more to the quality of Irish life than is dreamt of in the pages of the *Economist*, which is why many people who could improve their material standard of living elsewhere still chose to live here. They are concerned with trying to create a more open, tolerant, less fearful society in this country, while still not losing the qualities of generosity, embodied for example in the Constitution's commitment to the family. It would be a great pity if all this were to be lost sight of in the welter of arguments about the cost of tax cuts.

One senses, from time to time, that the politicians themselves are uneasy about the exclusively economic focus of the electoral debates, particularly as it has now become reasonably clear what differentiates the approaches of the major parties to the economy. Mary Harney made the point at the Progressive Democrats' press conference on Monday that there is more to their manifesto than cuts in public spending. Indeed there is, and some of it deserves to be explored more fully. Can I be the only person who now wonders whether, beneath that monetarist exterior there is a streak of the red revolutionary in Des O'Malley? Do all of his candidates agree with the laconic one-line proposal in the PD manifesto that the Senate should be abolished? What are the arguments for doing away with the second chamber which has in recent years provided a forum for Mary Robinson, Brendan Ryan, John Robb and Seamus Mallon? Perhaps the PDs have a convincing case but it would be nice to hear it.

Similarly with Garret FitzGerald. Has the Taoiseach now completely abandoned that mission which, he once told us, brought him into politics in the first place, i.e., to create a pluralist society down here that would make a Republic acceptable to the Unionists in the North? Given his experience of constitutional referenda and his Government's other clashes with the Catholic Hierarchy, it would be quite understandable if the constitutional crusade was now quite off the agenda. But many people voted for Fine Gael in the first place because Dr FitzGerald seemed to promise a vision of a more generous and tolerant country, and have the right to know if his party has abandoned that aspiration.

I have heard it said, rather gleefully by people who really should know better, that the liberal dream has died in the harsh realities of economic recession. If that is true and there is no room in this election for issues like women's rights, censorship, church–state relations, then our distress is greater than we thought.

Some facts of Irish life
always with us

FEBRUARY 18, 1987

And now, for something completely different? No, alas, more like more of the same. Some facts of Irish life are always with us. On Thursday just as I was settling down for The Great Debate, pad and pencil at the ready to evaluate whether I should blame Garret for the size of the National Debt and just how irresponsible it was of Charlie to promise to maintain public spending at its present level as a proportion of GNP, there was a knock at the front door. Not a canvasser, they were all in front of their televisions watching TGD. This was a neighbour from down the street. She was apologetic for disturbing me so late at night, knew that I was probably working out the future economic fortunes of the country, but it was a bit of an emergency as somebody was ringing from the country looking for the phone number of the centre which could give her the telephone number of a clinic in London where her friend could get an abortion.

Since the Mr Justice Hamilton judgment against the Well Woman Centre and Open Door Counselling, the Well Woman Centre has been taking between 15 and 20 calls a day from pregnant women in frantic distress. They have had to turn them away. To do so is an abandonment of the service to Irish women which they were set up to provide and they feel a deep sense of guilt at refusing women who need help. But they also offer a lot of other useful services to clients who need them. Yet they cannot risk the kind of entrapment which brought them to court in the first place and would this time put them in the dock charged with breaking Mr Hamilton's ruling. The indomitable Ms Ruth Riddick has received over 400 calls from women since Open Door Counselling closed. Each one of these comes from a woman in a personal crisis who has nowhere else to turn.

There is, of course – as there was in England before the passing of the Abortion Reform Act in the early 1960s – a network of women so that there is always someone who knows someone who would have the name of a doctor known to be reasonably liberal and sympathetic, professionally reliable and, above all, not so astronomically expensive as to be beyond a working woman's reach.

Many individual women here will be able to provide a London telephone number to a woman in distress, but that is already loading her choice towards abortion. They will not be able to provide the counselling which enables the woman to look calmly at all the options available to her, evaluate the costs and benefits of each, the effects on her and on her relationships, not just in the short term, but over a lifetime.

Whoever gets elected today, the desperate calls from women in distress will continue. Given the economic pressures that fall on a woman who finds herself unwillingly pregnant, the numbers going to England for abortions are likely to increase rather than reverse.

I don't propose here to examine Mr Justice Hamilton's ruling in any detail since that has already been done exhaustively in this and other newspapers. Lawyers to whom I have spoken believe that it was virtually inevitable that he would rule against the clinics though they also say that the terms of his judgment are frighteningly wide-ranging. The fact is, that given the authority of a judgment handed down from the High Court Bench, it stretches way beyond the two clinics involved in the case and has already frightened other people.

Here is just one example. Just before the ruling officially took effect last month a couple of hundred protestors gathered on a bitter–cold afternoon of falling snow outside the Four Courts. They carried a banner which had, quite simply, the telephone number of a pregnancy advisory clinic in England. At the scene, photographers and television camera-men begged the women not to carry the banner. They were personally sympathetic to the protest, they said, but knew their newspapers and/or RTÉ would not carry a picture of women carrying a banner, which had on it a telephone number which might constitute a defiance of a High Court ruling.

And so indeed it turned out. The banner did not appear in a single newspaper or on television, not even, as had been suggested, with the offending telephone number blanked out. Lawyers had advised that to show the telephone number might be construed as counselling women how to procure an abortion, and that might lead to the media being prosecuted for contempt of court.

There will be other cases of this kind and other judgments, and what will the media do, then, in defence of free expression? At what point will doctors finally decide that it is safe in the Irish context for them to protest about the erosion of their professional relationship with their patients? It might happen when the IUD is ruled to be abortifacient, or perhaps when the use of the morning-after pill is declared illegal. Perhaps not even then. Just down the road from me, in the neighbouring constituency, Family Solidarity has handed out leaflets with the questions the organisation has asked candidates in this election to answer.

One asks whether he or she will support moves in the Dáil to repeal Barry Desmond's Family Planning Act which made it legal to sell contraceptives to teenagers and unmarried persons. Another asks if the candidate will support a Bill to make abortion referral a crime under statute law and a third wants "an effective curb on pornographic literature", more effective presumably than that currently practised by the Censorship Board which last week led to the banning of *The Joy of Sex*.

These campaigns will continue to try roll back social progress through the courts, the Dáil, schools. Sooner or later, we are going to have to pull ourselves together and organise to resist them.

Making the red poppy a symbol of division

NOVEMBER 11, 1987

I found the red poppy on my coat on Sunday afternoon, a few hours after the news came through about the bomb in Enniskillen. At first I couldn't think how it came to be there, then I remembered. I got it at the Old Bailey last week. On the way into Court No. 12 for the appeal of the Birmingham Six, I threw a few coins into a British Legion collecting box in exchange for the paper flower.

It should have been a small civility, the kind of thing one does in Grafton Street as young people collecting for charity shake their boxes insistently for coins. It wasn't, of course, that simple. Even in the sterile atmosphere of the Old Bailey the poppy was a symbol. By buying it, I demonstrated to the security police on the door that I wasn't likely to be carrying an IRA bomb in my handbag. Inside the court, the division between those who did and didn't wear a poppy was almost complete.

The British – judges, lawyers, court officials – all wore in their lapels a red flower for remembrance. Nobody on the Irish side did, not the politicians nor the priests. Only the American observers who were there in sympathy with the six Irishmen in the dock wore their poppies quite naturally. But then the Americans do not regard Remembrance Day as exclusively British. It commemorates those who died in two world wars, no matter where they come from.

I used to feel that too. When I lived in England, even when I was reporting some of the worst of the violence in the North, I wore a poppy on Remembrance Day as a matter of course. Like thousands of other Irishmen, my father served in the British Army during the war and we never thought of him as less Irish because of that. It has always seemed to me to be one of the sadder episodes in our island history, not only that political expediency kept Ireland out of the war against Hitler, but that we still try to justify de Valera's condolences to the German ambassador on his death.

How much we limit ourselves and the part we have played in Europe's history by denying the Irish men and women who fought in both world wars. How pitiable that we think it will diminish the sacrifices made by those who died on Irish soil for independence if we recognise fully that other Irish people shed their blood in other fields.

We have heard the arguments, over and over again, as to why it would be inappropriate for the Government to be represented officially at any of the Remembrance Day ceremonies that are conducted by Irish men and women, commemorating their dead. We are told that in the North this is an exclusively Protestant occasion which, almost as much as July 12th, celebrates the Ulster Unionists' commitment to Britain. It has been said that the attack at Enniskillen was a deeply provocative act because it was directed at the Protestant community as it commemorated not the strutting victory of the Boyne, but the death and sacrifice of the Somme. Even if the Provos' statement is factually correct, and the bomb was timed to go off later and kill "Crown forces" after the Remembrance Day ceremony, it was still directed at an occasion celebrating one of the most sacred moments of

Ulster Protestants' history. The equivalent would be a bomb deliberately placed to go off at Bodenstown or during a parade commemorating the Easter Rising.

The tragedy demands a response from the political leaders of Irish nationalism that goes beyond mere condemnation of the bomb attack. It was Irish nationalists, first in the Forum Report and then in the Anglo-Irish Agreement, who invented the rhetoric about respecting both traditions in this island and put that concept on the political agenda. The main achievement of the agreement was that Britain accepted that it was necessary to create a framework which would enable both communities in Ireland to live together, respecting each other's traditions.

Yet in this part of Ireland, where it poses no threat, we have still to come to terms with the Remembrance Day poppy and what it commemorates. Last Sunday, in line with official policy, there was no formal Government representation at the Service in St Patrick's Cathedral. The ceremony itself took place several hours after the bomb exploded at Enniskillen. Yet, even at that moment of shock, nobody thought or dared to suggest that the most dramatic way the Irish Government could distance itself from this act committed in the name of the Irish people would be to send a Government minister to the service at St Patrick's.

If they really mean what they say about respecting both traditions, then our politicians are going to have to start taking risks to put flesh on their own rhetoric. A little common humanity in their responses to events north of the Border would help for a start.

It is extremely difficult to understand why no Irish minister has been sent to visit the injured or to represent the Government at the funerals of those who were killed in Enniskillen, as would have happened if the dead had been Catholics. Of course, it might cause offence, though I doubt it.

The impression that one gets in all the reports from Enniskillen is of a community in a state of numbed shock, grateful for any sympathy.

Would Mr Wilson, who spoke of his daughter's death on radio and television, have turned any mourner away from her funeral, or felt offended because that compassion came from Dublin? I don't think so. It would, anyway, be easy to discover about people's sensitivities by putting out feelers in advance.

Nobody doubts that Mr Haughey, like most of the people whom he represents, is appalled by what happened in Enniskillen or that he wants to hold out a hand of friendship to Northern Protestants. Somebody is going to have to start thinking about how best he can do that, in human as well as political terms.

1988

Hume and Adams and historical resonances

JANUARY 20, 1988

Neither John Hume nor Gerry Adams is giving much away about their meeting in west Belfast last week. Both men insist that there is no question of an alliance between the SDLP and Sinn Féin, that what took place was a free and frank exchange of views about the respective positions of the two parties in relation to the present situation in the North. Further dialogue between them is not ruled out, should either of them consider that it might be useful.

When Parnell met the Fenian leader, John Devoy, in 1879 both men were cautious about what had passed between them. Parnell was, characteristically, noncommital. Devoy was insistent that there was no alliance between them and no question of the Fenians abandoning their ideal of winning an Irish Republic through force of arms. Parnell did not volunteer, nor did Devoy press him as to what his own preferred political settlement would be. It made sense that there should be some dialogue between men representing the two most important strands in Irish nationalism to see whether they might work, if not for the same objectives, at least in the same direction. We know now the profound effect the New

Departure had on British policy towards Ireland and in convincing Gladstone of the necessity of Home Rule.

History does not repeat itself. But both John Hume and Gerry Adams are sensitive enough to the past to know what resonances their meeting must have had for anyone watching the progress of Anglo-Irish relations. The same is true of Mr Haughey, who knew of their meeting before it took place. All three men probably agree with Parnell's comment: "We shall never gain anything from England unless we tread upon her toes."

At the very least, the meeting signalled that the SDLP and Sinn Féin now share sufficient common ground that they would prefer not to regard each other as enemies to be mistrusted in private and attacked at every opportunity in public. The current issue of *An Phoblacht*, in an article analysing the talks, sets out the different political positions of the two parties in relation to a settlement in the North. What is notable about the article is not so much its content as its tone. This is calm and unhysterical, quite different from the abusive attacks which have been more characteristic of the paper's treatment of Hume in the past.

There are good reasons for both men to want the talks. Several times in recent months, Adams has said that there cannot be a purely military victory in the North. Those who support him have taken considerable risks within their own movement to pursue a political path, but have not achieved the breakthrough for which they hoped, particularly in the Republic. The organisation in the South has been particularly demoralised by Enniskillen. That atrocity has also raised serious questions about the methods employed to run their military campaign. Twenty years is a very long time and there must be real worry about how much longer the IRA and Sinn Féin can keep going in a situation where victory seems as remote as ever.

The fact that Sinn Féin has failed to win any significant degree of popular support in the Republic also makes its members feel particularly vulnerable to the present Government, should Mr Collins and his Department decide to move punitively against the organisation.

Sinn Féin leaders concede that the talks with Hume have caused some alarm at grassroots level that this may be the beginning of yet another "sellout" to constitutional national-ism, but Adams has been helped by the fact that those capable of articulating this suspicion have already departed for Republican Sinn Féin. He has been careful to carry his close aides with him and to explain himself at every step. They agree with his analysis that it is essential to give Sinn Féin's exhausted supporters some reason to hope that political movement is possible, and that they are not doomed to spend the next 20 years in a political isolation ward in their own country.

Hume, for his part, knows that the Provisionals are not going to go away as long as Northern Catholics living in the ghetto areas continue to believe that they are being discriminated against. He is realistic enough to accept that the Anglo-Irish Agreement has not brought the changes on the ground for which he and they hoped. On the contrary, it could be argued that one unwelcome effect of the agreement has been to leave the most deprived Catholics in the Bogside and the Falls feeling even more isolated from the mainstreams of Irish nationalism than they did before it was signed. Prior to Hillsborough they knew that at least there was widespread concern at the highest levels in Dublin about their grievances in relation to policing in the North and other issues.

Now there is a fairly general perception south of the Border that the agreement dealt with those problems and that all Northerners are alike, never satisfied. The feeling that the Republic has ceased to care has been underlined just recently by the debate on the fiftieth anniversary of the Constitution, and the proposal that the territorial claim on the North – and by extension, the moral claim to be concerned about it – should be dropped. In this context, it's not surprising that very many Northern Catholics, have been pleased to see their two extremely able leaders in apparently amicable dialogue, and a reminder sent to the British Government that the nationalist tradition in Ireland embraces two quite distinct strands, both of which have to be recognised if a lasting peace is to be achieved.

There are other political implications. The Anglo-Irish Agreement, of which Mr Hume is both architect and guardian, comes up for review before the end of the year. There is little sign that anyone in the Republic is devoting the necessary creative energy to thinking about where the review should lead. The Unionists are brooding, seriously, about their future but there is no evidence that they are yet in any mood to make the great political leap forward that might bring a lasting settlement. If and when that time does come, it is important that the Provisionals, who have it in their power to block any proposals, should be brought into political play. That will be easier if they are already engaged in some form of dialogue with Mr Hume which will enable Irish nationalism to present a coherent front.

It would be absurd at this stage to speculate on any long-term master plan. When Parnell met with John Devoy in Boulogne, neither of them was clear how this tentative alliance, which both denied existed, would work in practice. What breathed life into their new departure was the disastrous summer of 1879, the fear of another famine and events in Mayo. Neither the Fenian journalist in New York nor the Anglo-Irish landlord foresaw that it would be an organisation devoted to agrarian agitation that would transform their partnership and the course of Anglo-Irish history.

Could any of us have shouted "Stop"?

MARCH 23, 1988

They both wore the same shade of green, vivid as tropical birds against the grey of the Belfast sky and the dark clothes of the mourners. Daniel McCann's widow walked behind the coffin of her husband and later stood beside his grave, the gallant green of her coat contrasting with the red clay of Milltown Cemetery. Grenades had just stopped exploding and youths were running towards where the sound of gunfire had come from but she seemed oblivious to it.

She was trying to put a small bouquet of flowers on her husband's coffin in the grave, which had been dug to receive all three bodies, but it was too deep. Gerry Adams put his arm around her shoulders to steady her and helped her to place the flowers. Then the gravediggers started filling in the earth.

I saw the same jade green two days later. It was the colour of the thick sweater the young soldier was wearing when they dragged him onto the pavement and into Casement Park. His face was covered with blood, red as the cemetery clay. A dark, handsome lad in a chainstore sweater, he could have passed for one of the crowd in the funeral procession. He might even have escaped if he and his companion had parked their car and simply joined the mourners.

How did we let it happen? He passed within a few feet of myself and dozens of other journalists. He didn't cry out, just looked at us with terrified eyes as though we were all enemies in a foreign country who wouldn't have understood what language he was speaking if he called out for help.

Later, it seemed like hours but was in fact minutes, I found myself in a bookmaker's shop phoning for an ambulance. Someone in the shop said to me: "If anyone had tried to stop it, they'd have been killed too."

Now, several days later, I wonder. Probably we couldn't have prevented their deaths but we might, if we'd made a frenzy of the crowd, given some of them the moments they needed to become individual human beings again, responsible for their own actions.

Nobody, at least as far as I could see, tried. Not the bystanders, nor the journalists who were at less serious risk. Not Gerry Adams who, two days earlier, had cradled a widow's grief. There were priests in the crowd but not even they could stop a mob bent on lynching.

Heaven knows I'm not blaming them. Whenever in the future I see that green in a girl's dress or on a summer beach, I will have to ask why I did not make some gesture to show the young man in the green sweater that he was not utterly alone in a hostile country.

We all let it happen. The people of west Belfast are not "bestial", "savage", "barbaric", to repeat a few of the adjectives that have been applied to them. To suggest that they are is as offensive as some of the recent comments in the British press, to the effect that the Irish as a race are congenitally violent.

Last Saturday, west Belfast was a community in a state of nervous crisis unimaginable to most of us. All week, its people had walked to the cemetery behind the coffins of their dead or watched from the side of the road as the funerals passed. It was not a matter of their supporting the IRA, although undoubtedly many of them do just that. To many more, the young men and women who were buried were a part of their community. What filled the television screens were the paramilitary trappings of their funerals. But at the Requiem Masses I attended, local priests spoke of more homely things – membership of a football team, kindness to a handicapped child, religious devotion – the qualities any group of people recognises in its neighbours' children.

On top of their communal grief last Saturday, they feared, as did all who were present, that what was happening was another attack of the kind that had killed three people and injured dozens of others when Daniel McCann and his companions were buried.

Before the letter writers reach for their pens, I am not excusing the killing of the soldiers and need no lectures on ambivalence from people who condemn what happens in the North from the unambiguous comfort of an RTÉ studio at Montrose. I am suggesting that the blame does not lie only on the crowd who ran amok last Saturday, but on many of the rest of us who have left this community increasingly abandoned in recent years.

The sense of isolation in west Belfast and in similar Catholic ghettos of the North has, if anything, increased since the Anglo-Irish Agreement was signed thee years ago. That may not have been intended but it is the way it has turned out. These people have been excluded from the reasonable, moderate consensus of the accord. They vote Sinn Féin, elect a Sinn Féin MP and it has been made quite clear to them that this expression of political views, albeit conducted through the ballot box, puts them outside the pale as far as the body politic in the Republic is concerned.

At least before the agreement was signed, the Irish Government drew no distinction between good and bad members of the nationalist minority, welcoming those who voted for constitutional nationalism and rejecting the others. They were all "our people" and if that description excluded the Unionists, it was a failure which politicians in the Republic tried to address in the Forum Report.

Now, instead of the Unionists, we have categorised those who live in west Belfast and places like it as political and sometimes even moral lepers. In Dáil Éireann every political leader speaks of the need to woo and reassure the Unionists. I have done it myself in this column and will do so again. It's a very long time indeed since any of us spoke of wooing the people of west Belfast and drawing them back into the mainstream of the nation. On the contrary, there are complaints that RTÉ devotes too much time to the North. A journalist is sacked because a feature on *Morning Ireland* allowed Martin McGuinness to speak perhaps 200 words about arrangements for Mairead Farrell's funeral.

We now face the prospect of reaping the whirlwind.

The people of west Belfast showed us last weekend just how, if they are driven far enough, they will look after themselves. What happened on Saturday was not the work of the Provos, though many people would like to believe that relatively comforting theory. The IRA may in the end have shot the soldiers, but Sinn Féin was as powerless as anyone else in the crowd to control the lynching that led to their deaths.

Even if we would like to, we cannot write off Belfast as a place apart, isolate a community of 90,000 people as outlaws. We have to bring them and the political leaders who represent them in from the cold, give them some hope that progress is possible and that is will include them. It is a task of the greatest urgency for an Irish Government, more important even than repairing the state of Anglo-Irish relations.

A political necklacing for Haughey?

JULY 27, 1988

At the time of writing, the Taoiseach has still not given the promised press conference to report on what appears to have been a very successful trip to Australia. Everybody knows why or, what often amounts to the same thing in politics, thinks they know. Mr Haughey, it is said, does not want to answer questions about the gift of a diamond necklace presented to his wife by Crown Prince Abdullah of Saudi Arabia. The problem will not be resolved by avoiding reporters. Unless he takes steps to make it clear that the necklace is, of course, the property of the State, the Taoiseach could find that the damage the jewels do to his reputation will last as long as the aftermath of the Arms Trial. The saga of these diamonds could be forever.

A combination of circumstances – the Dáil recess, the appalling catalogue of tragedy from the North, the continuing circus of the Dublin Millennium – has meant that Mr Haughey has had a relatively easy time over the Saudi diamonds, so far. Added to this, there has been a reluctance on the part of the media to wound Mrs Haughey. Such sensitivity is commendable but, in this particular case, beside the point. Despite the Crown Prince's protestations of personal affection and respect for Mrs Haughey, the fact remains that the necklace was given to her because she is the wife of the Taoiseach, the elected head of the Irish Government.

Nobody seriously believes that Mrs Haughey would keep the diamonds if her husband told her to hand them over to the State. It is a measure of the regard that the Irish media and the public feel for her that the very idea of Maureen Haughey demanding to hang on to the jewels while CJ tries to wrest them from her is simply ludicrous. That hasn't been true of all political wives here or abroad. If anything, one senses a sympathy for a woman, who has always maintained a resolute public dignity over the years, that she should have been placed in such a position.

The political implications of the Crown Prince's diamonds are both domestic and foreign. It is axiomatic that there is no such thing as a free lunch in politics, much less a free diamond necklace. A gift of this magnitude, however delicately presented, is expected to influence Ireland's position in situations where the Saudis may look to this country for support – for example, when the turbulent situation in the Gulf is being debated. Nobody wants to spell it out, but the necklace and the other gifts are *baksheesh* or, in old fashioned Anglo-Saxon, a bribe against future difficulties. That is why countries who take their position in international affairs rather more seriously than we do, like the United States and Britain, have stringent rules about the gifts that politicians and their relatives may accept.

We may be sure that the gift has already been presented in this light by every embassy in Dublin that has had to report on the controversy to its Foreign Ministry at home. There will be another gloss in these reports in countries which have been, well, surprised, by the new, improved Mr Haughey and by his performance as a tough, responsible leader since the election. The British establishment in particular will derive considerable gleeful satisfaction from this evidence that the old, familiar, "Hukey" Haughey has not quite been laid to rest in the conversion to fiscal and other forms of rectitude. I, for one, would not like to be a minister or official representing this country at today's meeting at the Anglo-Irish Conference, conscious of the sniggers that have been directed at our Government over the Saudi gifts.

But the real damage will be done, where it matters, at home. It isn't necessary to linger on the use to which the diamonds could be put if, as reports indicate, they are worth somewhere in the region of $250,000. That sum could almost clear the debts that threaten the Rape Crisis Centre and would ensure its survival. It would open a hostel for homeless teenagers in inner-city Dublin, a group whose plight has been emphasised again in Focus Point's latest report. It could help to save the Irish consulate in Boston, which offers a priceless safety net to young illegal immigrants and which has been named as one of the missions targeted for closure in the latest cutbacks at the Department of Foreign Affairs. Every area in the country could put forward candidates for special consideration of this kind.

I know that it does not work like that, and that if the diamonds are declared to be the property of the State their value will not be used in this way. Nonetheless, the presentation to and acceptance of such expensive gifts by public figures will still be perceived in this way by every social agency struggling to survive in the present economic climate.

It is in this area, of the public's perception of the conduct of Irish politics, that the real damage will be done if the Crown Prince's necklace and the other gifts presented at Iveagh House remain in the hands of individual politicians.

It has always been part of the mythology surrounding the Taoiseach that the voters rather admire him for being a self-made man, who made a fortune by means that have never been subjected to effective public scrutiny. The popular suspicion that he might have cut a few corners along the way is believed, if anything, to have increased his popularity with the ordinary punter, who hoped Mr Haughey might bring the same Midas touch to the economy as he has to his own affairs.

That may have been true in the boom years of the late 1960s when the future looked rosy with the promise of eternal economic growth. It no longer applies today. Mr Haughey himself has been to the forefront in demanding a new rigour in the conduct of our financial affairs and has been widely applauded for his stance. He has asked people to make sacrifices in the name of patriotism, in order to get the economy straight and to guarantee a future for the nation's children.

For thousands of our people this has meant and continues to mean living on the breadline with little hope that things will get better in the immediate future. Astonishingly, many of them have responded to the call, have tried to survive without defrauding either the social welfare or, if they are lucky enough to be employed, the Revenue Commissioners. They have done so at least in part because this effort to come to grips with our chronic economic problems has resurrected a national sense of self-respect, a belief that as a nation Ireland could deal with hard economic realities while preserving a valuable social consensus.

Before this year is over, the Taoiseach will almost certainly go on television to explain that even harder sacrifices will have to be made if there is to be light at the end of the tunnel, and to appeal for people's confidence in his policies. Will he be able to do that – and how will people respond – if his wife is still wearing Crown Prince Abdullah's diamonds?

A remarkable resilience gives hope

AUGUST 31, 1988

Last week's issue of *An Phoblacht* carried an article about British media reaction to the Ballygawley bomb which killed eight young soldiers. There is a collage of newspaper headlines ("Lock Up the Bloody IRA Bastards" – *News of the World*), which gives the impression of a demented British press baying for internment. Whatever about the editorial in the *News of the World*, that isn't quite what happened last week.

On the contrary, every serious British newspaper and most of the populars ruled out internment, as did the vast majority of politicians with practical experience of the North, from Enoch Powell through to Ted Heath. More importantly, by the end of the week it appeared that Tom King had won the argument and convinced Mrs Thatcher that, though draconian security measures might seem attractive to the Victor of the Falklands, they would have disastrous consequences on the streets of Belfast and Derry. What the outcome of yesterday's killings near Omagh will be, of course, remains to be seen.

The bombing of the army coach at Ballygawley was as horrible as anything we have seen over the past few months. The descriptions of eyewitnesses who arrived on the scene in the early hours of the morning and had to gather up the bodily remains of the young soldiers were piteous.

And yet, perversely perhaps, the most striking impression one still retains from the last few months is how stable the community in Northern Ireland has managed to remain. This remarkable resilience on both sides, the apparent determination to resist the slide into broader sectarian conflict does provide a solid basis for the lingering hope that a moment of political opportunity exists which must be seized before further and worse violence blows it away.

Consider the reactions of the Unionist community in the North to the violence of this summer. While individual political leaders have been calling for the introduction of internment and/or other measures, the community as a whole knows that this is not a realistic or even desirable option. They remember not just what happened when internment was last introduced, but, much more to the point, the way communal tensions escalated during the period of the hunger strikes. They know that internment would give the Provisionals the issue they need – and which extradition has failed to provide – to organise mass protests on the streets. It would provide a single, simple political focus for Sinn Féin and deflect attention from the serious debate that is now going on within the party about its whole political direction.

The IRA has promised more and worse violence and nobody in the higher echelons of the security forces, on either side of the Irish Sea, doubts its present capacity to deliver on at least some of its threats. To some observers, particularly in Britain, it seems that the Provos now hold the initiative to dictate the bloody progress of events and that both Governments are equally powerless to stop them.

But the IRA does not operate in a political vacuum. For the moment, at least, it is committed to the dual strategy of the ballot box and the Armalite, which means that it has to keep one bit of an eye on the electorate. Otherwise, its leaders believe, it may just possibly win the war but will have no part to play in the shaping of the peace. In the shorter term, it is dependent on the tolerance, at the very least, of the Catholic community in areas like west Belfast and the Bogside. While this community has become fiercely, defensively loyal over the past 20 years, its support is not totally unconditional.

We need to understand that from the Provo point of view the concentration of the IRA's recent campaign on British soldiers has "political" advantages that go beyond the fact that the propaganda impact on British opinion is much greater than if it had killed equal numbers of RUC men and off-duty members of the UDR. The fact that it is British soldiers who have died, rather than locally recruited forces, is a major reason why the community in the North itself has remained relatively calm in recent months. The distinction is offensive. But it is real to the IRA.

Now, if we are to believe statements recently published, the IRA has, with the virtual stroke of a pen, extended its concept of "legitimate targets" so that almost anybody who works in the public service (security guards, elderly building workers, court officials) may be included in its sights. If this new campaign of terror goes ahead, it seems almost inevitable that people will be killed who, even in the twisted shorthand of Northern Ireland violence, will be widely regarded as "innocent". Similarly with the threat to bomb "economic" targets, which most commentators have taken to mean the placing of car bombs in city-centre streets.

Even allowing for the Provisionals' access to sophisticated explosives and their skills in using more accurate timing devices, the threat to the lives of "civilians" will be dramatically increased. At a more trivial level, the quality of life of many ordinary families will be even further limited if they are no longer able to enjoy the harmless pleasures of shopping and strolling in the revitalised city streets of Derry and Belfast.

All these threats, serious and not so serious, will cause

appalling suffering if they are carried out. They will also carry possibly intolerable political costs for Sinn Féin. At the most serious level, we already know that there is a serious debate going on within the Provisionals as to how their movement should relate to the Protestant community in the North. John Hume may not have convinced the IRA leadership that the best way to achieve their political objectives is by uniting Catholic, Protestant and Dissenter, but he has made many ordinary members uncomfortably aware that Sinn Féin has an historic duty to address the task set by Tone. How will these people react if more and more elderly building workers are blown to bits on the Border in the name of Irish unity?

What everybody in Northern Ireland needs desperately just now is some glimmer of hope that political progress may be possible. The effect would be profound even, particularly, indeed, within the ranks of the Provisionals themselves. At the moment, the political parties are paralysed and prevented from talking to each other by the violence, what has happened in recent months and may happen in the immediate future. Nobody seriously believes that talks about devolution are a serious possibility in the present security atmosphere.

Tom King has done a better job than most of his predecessors in holding the situation stable and in building a working relationship with Dublin which has helped to make the Anglo-Irish Agreement a reality. But there is no credible political initiative he can take on his own, and Mrs Thatcher, it seems, cannot see beyond the problems of security. As so often in recent months, it comes back to Mr Haughey. Just as Dublin provided the political energies and skills which brought the Anglo-Irish Agreement into existence, the present Taoiseach is the only politician who has even the possibility of moving the situation forward. How and when he should do it is a subject to which we will, God willing, return.

Tax dodgers rush in from the cold

OCTOBER 12, 1988

Here's a question for the end-of-term examination paper in Civics: "Patriotism is paying your taxes on time. – Discuss in the light of the recent tax amnesty."

The spectacular result of the amnesty has taken everybody by surprise, particularly – and this is interesting – the politicians. Ray MacSharry in his Budget speech estimated that the offer to tax dodgers to come in out of the cold might bring in £30 million. By the beginning of September, it had become obvious to accountants who were handling most of the money that this was a wildly erroneous forecast. Last week, the Department of Finance, sounding rather stunned, conceded that the take might be as great as £400 million. On Saturday, Mr MacSharry announced a final figure of £500 million.

Nobody has yet accounted for the difference between Mr MacSharry's original estimate, made presumably on the expert advice of his officials at the Department of Finance, and that final figure. Yet the gap is so stunning that it must, surely, tell us something about the state of the national psyche.

We have been accustomed to thinking of ourselves as a nation of dedicated tax dodgers, eager if at all possible to cheat the system at every turn. What if that is no longer true? Does the result of the tax amnesty signal a major change in national attitudes and, if so, how has that come about?

Those politicians who were always sceptical about a tax amnesty insist that nothing has changed. Barry Desmond and Tomás Mac Giolla see the figure as confirming their belief that there is widespread and continuing tax evasion among the self-employed.

Mr Desmond was quoted in the *Sunday Tribune* as saying that PAYE workers must now feel "totally cheesed off at the extent of tax evasion going on in other sectors of the economy". No rejoicing there over the scale of repentance among those sinners who have decided, albeit belatedly, to render what is owed to Caesar. Mr Desmond seems to be implying that the PAYE workers might have had more to cheer about if the tax amnesty had been a total flop, an odd view from a former Minister for Health concerned about savage cuts in the social services.

For the rest of us, the most striking thing about the £500 million must be the number of people who wanted to pay the taxes they owed and went to considerable pains to do so. Accountants to whom I've spoken confirm the general impression that the vast bulk of the money does not come from hardened tax dodgers making returns for the first time but from individuals, working on their own or running small businesses, who wanted to make up past arrears.

Far from glorying in their success at not paying their full tax in the past, they were deeply worried. Most of them had to borrow heavily in order to pay their debts within the time limits of the amnesty. Quite right, too, you will say, but this hardly accords with conventional pictures of the social parasite only too ready to let the unfortunate PAYE earner subsidise the social services from which he and his family also benefit.

Practically, the amnesty seems to have worked for a number of reasons. The self-interest of those who paid up was an important factor, but not the only one which made it a success. The Revenue Commissioners employed a judicious carrot-and-stick approach which appealed to the kind of people who were worried that over the years they had been a bit, well, casual about their taxes. There was more than a hint of "Pay now and we'll try to be understanding; leave it and you don't know when we'll get you or for how much".

The introduction of self-assessment has also, it seems, changed people's attitudes. When it was first suggested, there was a scepticism that it would be a tax dodger's charter. Instead, it has been a success, demonstrating once again that if you treat people as adults and put on them the onus of meeting their social responsibilities, most of them will do just that.

This in itself marks a shift in social attitudes which is worth remarking upon, maybe even celebrating. When I first returned to live in Ireland in the mid-1970s it was quite common to meet people who boasted quite openly about their success in not paying any income tax over a number of years. The connection between their failure to pay tax and, say, the appalling standard of some social services was never made.

It seems just possible that that too has changed. At the very least, it does not seem to be fashionable any more to brag about not paying taxes. This must owe something to the much greater public awareness of the harsh economic facts of life. In recent years, the magnitude of this country's economic problems has become generally accepted as something in which we are all involved. Those who have a job or are able to make a living in Ireland know that they are very lucky.

As well as this, the demonstrations and marches organised by the trade unions have taught us that the PAYE sector does bear a quite disproportionately heavy and unfair part of the tax burden. People have been forced to make the connection between the kind of public services the Government provides and its ability to raise revenue through taxes. They know, though they may not always admit, that the state of affairs in Temple Street Hospital is not due to any lack of humanity on the part of the Minister for Health. It is the result of lack of funds in the Exchequer.

The National Debt affects all of us and our children. For all these reasons, it is no longer quite so socially acceptable to talk of cheating the Revenue Commissioners as though they were oppressive tax collectors representing absentee land-lords or an alien state.

I can even now hear the distant letter writers sharpening their quills to explain that all this is impossibly naive and that there still exist very many people in this country who will continue to regard tax evasion as the most challenging art form unless very heavy sanctions are imposed to deal with them.

That may be true but the amnesty does demonstrate that most people are quite willing to pay their taxes even when they are heavy, if they believe them to be fair and reasonable. What is shocking is that to so many people who govern us – politicians and civil servants – this has come as a huge surprise.

1989

Examining roots of Ulster loyalism

MAY 17, 1989

A Gem of a movie, caught just after midnight on Channel 4, deserves a wider audience. I hope that it will at least get a showing on RTÉ.

We'll fight and No Surrender focused on the tercentenary of the Siege of Derry, to look at the Protestant community that remains within the walled city and to examine what that first, treasonable act of defiance against an anointed king meant to Northern Protestants then and now. At one level it was an intimate, affectionate portrait of a community that has always felt itself under attack in its own city, vulnerable to the natives outside the walls and unable to trust the English relief forces, dallying incomprehensibly at the mouth of Lough Foyle while those under siege starved.

But besides, *We'll fight and No Surrender* was a piercing examination of the roots of Ulster loyalism, the psychology of a people trapped in an historic scenario not of their making, clinging to the past because they see no hope for the future.

Writer Desmond Bell looked at the class origins of the siege and the importance these have assumed in Protestant working-class mythology – the treachery of the Anglicised officer, Lundy, contrasted with the humble origins of the Apprentice Boys, "sturdy, loyal and true".

He was particularly good on the young today, a generation

which cannot even remember the recent past when a Unionist minority controlled Derry city and used their patronage to deliver jobs and houses to their own. In Derry now, the young men who make up the only flute band left on the West Bank are not apprenticed to a trade. Unemployed, they join the band because it provides something to do, keeps them together, bolsters a faltering sense of belonging to a community.

In recent years, Catholics have reclaimed the site of the city within the walls, rebuilding the eighteenth-century houses and painting the shop signs in Gaelic letters. There is even a fort recreated to the memory of the rebel chieftain, O'Doherty. The intentions may be of the best but to the Protestants the message is clear and borne out by the physical conditions under which they live.

The numbers of their community have declined and the Fountain estate is guarded by a high, spiked fence – walls within walls. Here, even the rich and gorgeous murals of King Billy on his white charger, which the Jackson family have painted for generations, are locked behind steel shutters, and opened only for special occasions when the tribe celebrates its history.

Rarely for a television crew, the cameras were allowed inside the museum of the Apprentice Boys hall, lingering on tattered banners and family photographs from days gone by. "It is a strange, jumbled collection," the narrator commented, "part regimental display, part family china cabinet filled with intimate memories of the past." The film used these mementos to explain and illuminate the present dilemma of the Protestant community, a people to whom the past seems increasingly seductive as the future becomes ever more uncertain.

As important as the content of *We'll fight and No Surrender* was the elegant, ironic assurance of its style. Desmond Bell, who wrote and directed, gave us a thought-provoking, literate script underpinned by the beautiful images of the city of Derry – its physical intensity, the faces of the siege victims in the stained-glass windows of the Guildhall, the wide sweep of the Foyle. These were juxtaposed with shots of the bands practising, the lament of a community for its past, the symbolism of the British Army on the walls.

There was an element of special pleading. The hatreds of the present were hinted at but in a way that made them seem almost witty rather than murderously life threatening. These days, the Relief of Derry is celebrated in Protestant areas by an *auto da fe* of Sinn Féin posters and, as the flames leapt upwards on screen, the director added the strains of the "Sanctus", reminding us that William of Orange's victory was celebrated with a thanksgiving mass in the Vatican.

There are other quibbles. Were Derry Protestants really so innocent of triumphalist attitudes to their fellow citizens in the bog? At least Mr Bell put such questions on the screen and may even have opened them to debate. He looked at the past and related it to the present and in this, perhaps, lies the main importance of his film.

Over the past 20 years, Northern Protestants have been depicted across the world as bigoted, ignorant of their own history, mulishly stubborn. The sense that they have never got a fair hearing has contributed to and reinforced the sense of paranoia, which is in itself an obstacle to progress. At one stage, it might have been argued that the Unionist case went by default because there was in reality no case to make, but if that was true 20 years ago, it is not so now.

Today the most urgent task for both communities in Ireland is to re-examine their mutually exclusive visions of the past and, in trying to come to terms with history, to reach a new understanding of the other's position.

In the Republic, that process is already under way. Some

argue that the revisionists have already gone too far and that, in the retreat from a nationalist view of history, we are in danger of jettisoning altogether a legitimate pride in the struggles of the past. Nonetheless, it is a debate which most people believe must be undertaken by all shades of nationalism in the interests of a better future.

There is an urgent need for the Unionist community to engage in the same process of re-examining its history, retaining a sense of pride for the sacrifices of the past but coming to accept that these do not provide all the answers for the future. At one stage in Mr Bell's film, the co-ordinator of a Derry committee, set up to try to devise ways of commemorating the siege that might involve both communities, says, "The message is that the siege is over."

That patently isn't true. The siege lives on in the hearts and minds of Northern Protestants. Mr Bell's film may have helped that community to look again at this most powerful parable of its past, and to ask what relevance it has to the sense of loss and betrayal experienced in recent years. Perhaps it may even lead some loyalists to the conclusion that if the past could only be laid to rest, they might face a brighter, albeit less exclusive, future.

Some things did change in 20 years

AUGUST 16, 1989

In the early summer of 1969, a pleasant Protestant matron in Derry poured me a second cup of coffee, pressed me to take a home-made scone and remarked: "But I'd never be operated on by a Catholic surgeon, would you? You couldn't be sure that he'd sterilise the instruments or wash his hands."

This woman was not politically extreme. Quite the reverse. She had been asked by her local clergyman to get a group of her friends together to talk to me, because he and his congregation were worried about the mounting crisis in the city. She knew it was wrong and deplored the fact that large Catholic families could not get houses because the local Unionist-controlled council was determined to deny them votes.

I had not intended to return in this column to the twentieth anniversary of the deployment of British troops on the streets in the North, for I accept Bishop Poyntz's admonition that we really must try to look to the future rather than the past. But the experience of spending last weekend in Derry, combined with the saturation coverage which the anniversary has received, is too provoking.

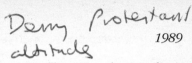

I will, honestly, try to ensure that this is my last work on then and now.

The general tone of the comments, here as well as in Britain, has been deeply negative. The London *Independent* just about summed it up with the headline "Twenty Dreadful Years". There has been an almost exclusive concentration on the death and suffering of two decades of violence, the physical polarisation of the two communities, the lack of political progress.

The speeches from what one might loosely describe as the Troops-Out side have been no less gloomy. Bernadette McAliskey was reported in this paper on Monday as saying that nothing had changed, that even winning one man, one vote had been meaningless.

I keep thinking of all those people whom I interviewed in Derry 20 years ago, on both sides of the community. I find it difficult to believe that very many of them would want to return to the *status quo ante* and to a situation which in its way degraded both Protestants and Catholics.

It was a time when both sides, from their different perspectives, believed that Catholics were second-class citizens, when discrimination was institutionalised not only at every level of the political system but ingrained in the attitudes of both communities.

I am not for a moment suggesting that the bigoted attitudes were the sole preserve of the Unionist/Protestant community. Catholics had their own stunning sense of superiority, based on the unswerving belief, inculcated from babyhood on, that they were God's chosen people.

But the Protestants had temporal power, knew they held it precariously in a state of siege and, like every group in that situation – whites in South Africa, Jews in Israel, men in relation to women – they needed constantly to convince themselves and others that it was part of the natural order of things that they should rule the roost.

Buried in the attic somewhere, I have a pile of notebooks from that period, containing interviews which reflect, over and over again, the kind of attitudes quoted at the beginning of this column. Most of the Protestants to whom I talked in Derry were not bad nor vicious, and were quite unselfconscious about their prejudices. That they talked to me at all, at a time when I was seen by most Protestants as a less than wholly objective supporter of the Civil Rights Movement, was an indication of their desire to reach outside the confines of their own community.

There was the liberal businessman who invited me to his lovely house overlooking the Foyle because he wanted to talk about the way the local Unionist Party was "destroying this city with their bigotry". He was in mid-tirade when a young, uniformed maid appeared. Immediately he put a finger to his lips and whispered "*Pas devant...*". Later, he explained that this cautionary gesture was because she was a Catholic.

A council official to whom I talked was genuinely appalled at the human suffering. On the other hand, he had to say that, honestly, he did not believe that nationalists would ever be capable of running the city.

There were other cruder articulations of prejudice about Catholics – their laziness, their talent for music, their sexual avidity – all very familiar to anyone who had read anything about the American South.

At the time, I had been commissioned to write a book about Derry, which was one reason I was talking to all these people. I never wrote it, mainly because the guilt and confusion of these Protestants was almost unbearable and there was no way I would be able to report on them without making them sound like appalling bigots, rather than people already sensing that all their certainties were about to be swept away.

But what all this did to the Catholic community has to be remembered too. We look back to the Civil Rights Movement now and see images of brilliant young leaders making dazzling speeches, of the defiance and bravado of a whole community ranged against the forces of an unjust State.

It was not all like that. Most Catholics in Derry and elsewhere were defeated by the stereotypes and accepted the underdog status which history had allocated to them. There were rich Catholics in Derry but on the whole they were successful in trades which Protestants thought beneath them – butchers, publicans, bookies. These in turn reinforced the image, for Catholics as well as Protestants, of a community of drinkers and gamblers.

It was taken for granted that no working-class Catholic would get a job with the local authority unless he was an ex-serviceman. The Butler Education Act had taken Catholics to university but no graduate could expect to rise high in the Civil Service. They might become lawyers and doctors but their chances of getting the top jobs on the Bench or in local hospitals were virtually non-existent.

It has often occurred to me since that one reason Northern nationalists clung so passionately to the South, which patently cared so little for them, was because they needed to know that Catholics could in fact govern themselves, run a democratic State, make a success of the civil service, behave impeccably as judges.

I will be reproached for raking over the past and it will be argued that all this would have changed anyway with greater material prosperity, access to education, the winds of change prevailing in the outside world. I wonder.

There have been very few places where those who held power have been willing to relinquish it until the dispossessed organised themselves to change the situation. There are even fewer where the deeply ingrained prejudices of those who want to believe they have a right to rule have been changed by peaceful persuasion alone.

In Northern Ireland, the Westminster Government has come under intense pressure, from quarters ranging from the Provisional IRA to international opinion, to institute reforms which most British ministers would now agree were overdue 20 years ago. Even so, the unemployment rate among male Catholics today is 36 per cent compared with 14 per cent for Protestants. That is some indication of how difficult it has been to achieve perfectly reasonable reforms.

But to say that nothing has improved in 20 years, that the toll of human suffering renders all progress meaningless, is as misleading as the Northern Ireland Office's glossy propaganda claiming that every grievance has been put right. A great deal has changed at an institutional level for the better. As important, the laws which have been passed and implemented have forced both communities to rethink very many of their traditional attitudes.

Northern Ireland 20 years ago was a society built on discrimination and sustained by prejudices fostered obsessionally on both sides. That is no longer true and we should recognise the fact with some gratitude.

A few days home may mark
the change

AUGUST 30, 1989

Well, the boys are back in jail. According to impeccable sources in Northern Ireland, some of them were already outside the prisons early yesterday morning, accompanied by what are euphemistically described as "their associates", waiting for the doors to open. The Northern Ireland Prison Service claims that it never seriously expected that any of the 143 life prisoners given four days' "home leave" over last weekend would break their parole. At Christmas, when 118 lifers were allowed to spend the holiday period at home, they all returned on time, including one who had passed the festive season at his sister's home in South Armagh, less than 100 yards from the Border.

There has been a deafening official response to what has certainly been the most hopeful – and may well be the most politically significant – news to come from the North in a very long time. The decision to allow the long-term prisoners – 66 republicans, 71 loyalists – this period of leave had already been taken before Tom King left Northern Ireland. It was one of the first things the new Secretary of State, Peter Brooke, announced just after he took office, partly to confirm to both communities with paramilitary prisoners in the jails, that he

73

intended to continue with the policies initiated by his predecessor.

Last Thursday, John Cope, the new Minister of State with responsibility for the prisons, explained that home leave of this kind "played an important part in the process of preparing prisoners who have spent a long time in prison for their eventual return to the community".

There may be a perfectly innocent explanation why the Irish Government has not commented on an initiative which surely falls within the scope of those interests covered by the Anglo-Irish Agreement. The Minister for Foreign Affairs is on holidays and his officials, who are paid to notice such things, may well be too. Perhaps they noticed, but did not think the temporary release of so many supposedly dangerous "terrorists" into the community worth remarking on.

It is just possible, though not, I fear, very likely, that the Government finds the whole thing rather embarrassing. This column has commented before on the contrast between the relatively enlightened approach of the British prison authorities in the North and that of successive governments in the Republic to the unfortunate life prisoners in Portlaoise, on whose behalf Cardinal Ó Fiaich, among others, has pleaded for some degree of clemency.

Political leaders on both sides of the North have welcomed, with some reservations, last weekend's initiative. But it has been left to Fr Denis Faul to describe it as "positive detailed work for peace". There are two reasons why the policy initiated last Christmas and continuing now under Peter Brooke's regime is politically important. The first is the argument on which Fr Faul himself has so long campaigned. There are sections of both communities in the North, but particularly those who live in the nationalist ghettos, who feel themselves profoundly alienated from the normal structures of society and, in particular, from all aspects of the administration of justice. It is a major reason why they continue to give their loyalty and support to paramilitary organisations. The single initiative, Fr Faul has argued, which might begin to reverse that process, by persuading them that their grievances are understood, would be to start releasing their sons and husbands, brothers and sisters, who are in prison. The British know, as we all should, that very many of these men and women, particularly those convicted of terrorist crimes committed in the early 1970s, would not be in prison at all were it not for the atmosphere of violence prevailing at the time.

But appeals to clemency, even to natural justice, are rarely effective in persuading those who control the prison system in any country, particularly if they believe that a degree of political risk is involved. That is why it is, at the very least, so interesting that the British have begun, ever so discreetly, the process of getting public opinion accustomed to the idea that the paramilitary "lifers" in Northern Ireland are ordinary men and women who will one day, quite soon, return to ordinary lives in their own communities.

Of all the many hours of television devoted to the twentieth anniversary of the deployment of the British troops, by far the most moving were the trilogy of films *Families at War*, made by Peter Taylor. And of that trilogy, the film which created the greatest impact in Britain was the first, *The Volunteer*, which told the story of and contained a long interview, filmed in prison, with the former IRA bomber, Shane Paul O'Doherty.

Of course the film could not have been made without the full co-operation of the prison authorities, and I've seen the suggestion made that it was clever anti-IRA propaganda, converted terrorist repents his evil deeds, etc. I was in England the week it was shown and, among the people to whom I spoke, that wasn't the impact it made at all. On the contrary, the message they took away from it was one which I do not believe the British authorities would have wanted presented even a year ago. This was that young men who get involved in the IRA are not the vicious thugs which they had always previously assumed. They and their families may be instead, normal, decent people caught up in a tragic situation which they have no power to control.

The British want the violence in the North to end. They know that there can be no progress until the paramilitaries on both sides, but particularly the Provisional IRA, can be persuaded to call off their campaign. Like anyone who reads *An Phoblacht* or listened carefully to the various speeches made up to and during the many Republican marches for the twentieth anniversary of the deployment of the troops, they know just how profound is the war weariness felt not just in the Catholic ghettos of the North, but in the Provisionals' own ranks.

But, because they are politically experienced in conflicts of this kind, the British also know that it is going to be extremely difficult for the Provisional leadership to move, even tentatively, towards ending their campaign. They cannot be seen to betray not simply the political ideal of a united Ireland, but also the suffering and sacrifices endured by their own membership over the past 20 years. In particular, they cannot abandon the prisoners who have given their liberty and, in the case of the hunger strikers, their lives, for the struggle. If any progress is to be made, the Provisional leadership must be given room to manoeuvre, concessions which they can present to their own supporters if not as outright victories, then as tangible evidence that the political attitudes of the British have changed.

Last weekend's few days' "home leave" and the conciliatory statements just might mark the first tentative steps along that road.

1990

Virgin takes risks on safe sex

MAY 23, 1990

Here is an intriguing dilemma now facing Mr Eamon Barnes. At what point should the Director of Public Prosecutions decide to haul Richard Branson into court for quite positively promoting the sale of "engines of fornication" (as condoms were once described in a famous disciplinary case at Oxford University) in his Virgin Megastore beside the Liffey.

Mr Branson – he of the hippy looks and marvellously eccentric enthusiasms – is one of Mrs Thatcher's favourite businessmen. His Virgin airline and his record stores were one of the huge successes of the 1980s.

His talent for publicity is legendary. Every time he goes up in a hot-air balloon he seems to prove that running a multi-million-pound business can be fun. But Mr Branson is more than a former boy wonder with an eye for a gap in the market. He has a social conscience. In Ireland this has been felt mainly through his crusade to do something positive about AIDS.

In May 1988, Mr Branson flew into Dublin to be present at the charity premiere of *Wall Street* and to present a cheque for £100,000 to the AIDS Action Alliance. Given the aura of fear, ignorance and Government distaste for the subject of AIDS, the money came as more than a generous gesture. It was a lifeline to those involved in research and treatment of the condition.

But Mr Branson did more than hand out money. He allowed the Irish Family Planning Association (IFPA) to set up a stall in the Virgin record store on Aston Quay, accepting their argument that condoms should be made easily available to those who needed them most – i.e. young people who were inhibited from buying them elsewhere by the state of the law, their own cultural conditioning and a powerful sense of embarrassment.

Everyone knew that there were legal risks involved but no attempt was made to persuade the IFPA to hide the stall away, or make it purposefully discreet. On the contrary, it is situated right in the middle of the first floor, beside the rock 'n' roll records, and is stylishly designed in black, white and red, with the Virgin logo prominently displayed.

When the first case against the IFPA was taken (and dismissed on a technicality) seven months ago, Mr Branson made it quite clear where he stood. Up to that time the stall had been open only on Saturdays because it was a commercial arrangement; the IFPA paid rent to Virgin and that was all they could afford.

Now, that was changed. Mr Branson told journalists that he found it almost incredible that at a time when most European countries were spending huge sums to try to persuade young people to use condoms, attempts were being made in Ireland to stop them. In future, the IFPA stall would be open six days a week, rent-free, in his store.

A survey carried out during two months of this year shows that, on average, a hundred people a week buy condoms at the stall. This increases at holiday weekends or when there is a big sporting event in Dublin, for example a major GAA fixture (!) or a rugby international.

There is also a rush of customers, particularly from the

country, when the stall has received publicity in the media, as happened last week. Ninety per cent of those who buy are men and the majority of those are under 25. It seems that the stall is reaching just the kind of client which health organisations concerned with AIDS all over the world are most concerned to target.

It may be true – and was certainly accepted as the truth in the District Court last week – that very many people who buy condoms at the Virgin stall do so to use them as contraceptives rather than to protect themselves against AIDS. If so, it means that at least a few more Irishmen, particularly young men, are taking their sexual responsibilities more seriously.

The defence put forward in court by counsel for the IFPA was that the condoms were being sold as prophylactics. The appearance of the stall, perhaps deliberately, supports this intention. There are posters urging "Safe Sex" and leaflets making the point that women are also vulnerable to AIDS, something borne out by recent research showing the increased incidence of the infection among heterosexuals.

After last week's verdict, Mr Branson drew the Taoiseach's attention to Ireland's role in the presidency of the EC. By one of those nice ironies which have happened quite a lot since January, a specialist group set up by the European Community to monitor the spread of AIDS was meeting in Dublin on the day that the decision against the IFPA was given in the District Court. Dr James Walsh, director of Ireland's AIDS programme, told the conference that the incidence of AIDS in this country is now doubling every 16 months. This rate of increase is very much higher than the European average although, of course, we start from a much smaller base. Professor Meinhard Koch, the chairman of the EC group, said that although initially there had been a great deal of media interest in the issue, it had tailed off and there was now a real danger that AIDS could become the "forgotten disease" in terms of public education and attention.

Noel Browne has compared Irish attitudes to AIDS to those which were, not so long ago, associated with tuberculosis. Ignorance, prejudice, fear, the attempt to ghettoise the condition by describing AIDS as "the gay plague" – all these not only cause terrible suffering to AIDS victims, but are extremely dangerous for society.

His point is taken up in a powerfully emotional documentary film *Voices from the Silence* (which will be screened on RTÉ on Thursday, May 31st) in which AIDS victims and their families talk about their experiences. Near the beginning there is a clip from a black-and-white film, made presumably in the 1940s or 1950s, in which a TB sufferer tells his mother of his condition. She cannot bring herself to call the illness by its real name but asks, delicately, whether his wife is "not strong" because of course, there was never anything like that "on our side of the family". The film, amid the very moving stories of human suffering and courage, is full of just such slights – the priest who asks for prayers from the pulpit for AIDS victims but cannot say the word itself, the doctor who tells a patient that he is "slightly positive", the appalling, open prejudice and suspicion.

By giving a human face to the terrifying initials, the film shows how inadequate our stereotypes are; all sorts and conditions of people are here talking about and demystifying their own experiences.

Launching the film, Noel Browne made the point that, just as happened with TB, the stigma and the superstition that surround AIDS will only be swept away by a programme of comprehensive health education. He didn't add, of course, that the reason this happened all those years ago with tuberculosis was that Ireland had a Minister for Health prepared to take on all the entrenched forces of the establishment who stood in the way of his achieving his object.

Dr Rory O'Hanlon is no Noel Browne, although he faces as formidable a challenge. He is a politician who will react to the pressures which he feels to be strongest. After all that has happened in recent months, I can hardly bear to say it, but it *is* up to the rest of us to keep reminding him that the needs of Irish society extend far wider than the demands of Family Solidarity.

A "Dear John" letter from Mary

MAY 30, 1990

An Open Letter to John Taylor

Dear John,

You'll forgive, I hope, the familiarity of this opening – after all we've known each other for more than 20 years now, even if we've disagreed quite often during that period. I hope, too, that you'll understand why I want to write this column in the form of an open letter, rather than pick up the telephone to talk to you about the parliamentary question you've tabled for Peter Brooke, asking the Secretary of State to raise the future of the Adelaide Hospital through the Anglo-Irish Conference.

I want to convey publicly the reactions I've had from people down here. I think you'd be amazed how many people – many of them women, most of them, nominally at least, Roman Catholics – have described your attempted intervention in our affairs as "brilliant". I can see a future for you down here as a liberal hero, John, a role I don't think either you or I would have predicted for you during most of the past two decades.

As I recall, you didn't like it much when journalists and others came nosing around County Tyrone back in 1968 asking questions about discrimination in housing, civil rights and how the Unionist Party ran Northern Ireland. But let's not get into all that.

I only mention it because you, of all people, should understand when political reaction down here to your questions about the Adelaide is rather cool. Don't let that put you off. As you say, if Dublin can claim the right to have a say about the way the nationalist minority in the North is treated then it's only fair that Unionists should be able to ask questions about minority rights in the Republic. Fair? It's fantastic. Why do you think so many people have mourned the absence of the Northern Protestant voice in the affairs of this State? A friend of mine rang this morning. He'd just been reading Family Solidarity's latest, *The Homosexual Challenge*. "Perhaps they're coming to help us now just when we need them most," he said, meaning the Unionists.

First, though, the Adelaide. To be honest, the Protestant Churches have been a bit mealy-mouthed about it. They keep talking in vague terms about "the Protestant ethos" of the hospital. To most people down here that means that operations like vasectomy and female sterilisation are performed at the Adelaide. Of course, that's important because it's extremely difficult to get these operations done in most Catholic hospitals, but you know that the Protestant ethos means a lot more than that.

In this context, it means that decisions about treatment are taken, after consultation between doctor and patient, on medical grounds, without the whole weight of Catholic moral teaching being brought into play through an ethics committee.

The influence of these committees on the practices in Catholic hospitals ranges from the trivial to the tragic. A doctor friend told me recently of sending a patient who had hurt her back to hospital for an x-ray. She was told to come back in a couple of weeks when she had had her monthly period. She protested that she knew as near as dammit that she was not pregnant. No dice. A minor inconvenience, but the same mode of thinking can mean the difference between life and death.

I don't know if you followed our "pro-life" referendum carefully enough to have read the truly harrowing story of Sheila Rodgers. An interview with her husband appeared in this paper, so I'll just recall it briefly. Sheila Rodgers was married with two young children when she was diagnosed as having breast cancer. She was put on a course of treatment and at the same time taken off the contraceptive pill. Nobody seems to have advised her about alternative methods of contraception and she became pregnant. The treatment for her cancer was discontinued as it might endanger the embryo; at the same time, the effect of the pregnancy was to accelerate the spread of the cancer through her whole body.

If she had lived in Britain, given the fact that she already had two children, the pregnancy would almost certainly have been terminated. This was not, of course, discussed. Instead, after several months of dreadful suffering which reduced her at times to screaming for some form of pain-killer she gave birth to a baby girl who died almost immediately.

A few days later, Sheila herself died in great pain. This case was well known within the medical profession but was never raised during the whole of the "pro-life" amendment campaign. That's how things work around here, whatever the suffering involved.

So, keep asking the questions about the Adelaide, John, but don't stop there. Might I suggest a number of issues for you to consider as possibly suitable for airing through the Anglo-Irish conference. Most of them have a British or a European dimension and they all raise questions about minority rights. At the very least, they will give useful employment to those civil servants who are left at Maryfield while the talks about "Peace in our Time" are progressing elsewhere.

1. **The Right to Information:** As you know, the Protestant Churches in the Republic were opposed to the amendment outlawing abortion, on the grounds that the teaching of one Church on moral issues of this kind should not be written into the constitution. They also argue that there are cases – e.g. rape, incest – when abortion should be considered as an option.

Since the referendum, the screws have been tightened relentlessly on attempts to provide counselling or information to women who find themselves unhappily pregnant. British magazines such as *Cosmopolitan* and *Company* have either been censored or threatened with being banned if they include advertisements or articles about abortion, no matter how even-handed.

Student leaders at Trinity and elsewhere are being held personally liable for the cost of cases taken against them in the courts by private groups, to stop them publishing information in their newspapers and handbooks.

Now it seems that an attempt to reverse this trend by the Well Woman Clinic and Open Line Counselling may, just possibly, be successful. The two clinics have had their appeal against the Supreme Court ruling of 1988 accepted for hearing by the European Court of Human Rights at Strasbourg. SPUC's comments on this, as yet, very small victory are revealing. A spokeswoman for the organisation is quoted in this week's *Catholic Standard* as saying that taking the case to Europe is "an exercise in futility" by the clinics, since even if the court at Strasbourg finds in their favour it will make no difference to Irish law.

The depressing thing about this, John, is that she is almost certainly right. That brings us on to:

2. **Homosexuality:** It is now two years since the European Court found in favour of David Norris but the Government appears to have no intention of changing the law so as to

decriminalise homosexuality. I know the same tortuous path had to be taken by gays in Northern Ireland and that many many Unionists were not too keen on the European ruling, but at least the law was changed.

There are other subjects – AIDS, availability of contraception to the young, sex education in schools, *in vitro* fertilisation – but I am running out of space. Besides, I have another engagement. I'm just off to hear Ian Paisley Junior address a meeting in Dublin about the Armagh Four.

I remember the late Harold McCusker telling me that he'd asked Irish politicians to look at the case of these four UDR men who claim that they are imprisoned for a murder they did not commit. I don't think he got much joy. "We're only Irish when it suits them," he said to me.

So, why not put it up to them? Believe me, there are a lot of people down here yearning to cheer you on. Enjoy the moral high ground; you could get to like it. I'll be in touch.

IRA brings anarchy
one stop nearer

OCTOBER 31, 1990

The publican had just come across a human arm in the glass and debris on the floor of his bar and was, understandably, a bit upset. "You think you've absorbed it, that you're lucky to be alive. Then something like this happens and it really gets to you." He had been allowed back into the pub at Coshquin, on the main Derry to Buncrana road, to pick up a few mementos – old photographs, a few sporting trophies, that sort of thing.

All around, in the watery sunshine, people were replacing windows and doors, doing repairs on the small houses that had been devastated by the blast that had killed five British soldiers and Patsy Gillespie, the Derryman who had been forced by the IRA to drive the car containing 1,000 lbs of explosives. Old-age pensioners welcomed us into their kitchens, apologised for not being able to offer a cup of tea, and pointed to where ceilings and glass had fallen on them as they slept. Outside, a young man in jeans with a rifle slung casually over his shoulder came up to us: "If you're going to the barrier, say a prayer for them. They were my soldiers." A little further down the road, against the iron scaffolding, there were wreaths and posies of garden flowers. Most of them

87

were for Patsy Gillespie, but almost all said, "For Patsy and the others who died with him".

As we walked away, an SDLP councellor said to me: "It puts taped interviews and all that into perspective, doesn't it?" For a moment, I couldn't think what he was talking about and assumed it must be something to do with procedures for questioning suspects picked up by the RUC. Then it dawned on me that he meant Brian Lenihan, whether or not he had made the telephone calls to the Park.

How distant all that seemed in Derry last week and how trivial compared to the shock and suffering on this little estate, situated in bleakly beautiful countryside just a couple of miles from Donegal. Except that, of course, it is important and immediately relevant because these people are so dependent on what is happening in politics south of the Border. Whoever gets to run things down here will affect their lives and their hopes for an eventual peace.

Human resilience means that life goes on. Houses get fixed, children are summoned home to funerals. The shock comes later. In Patsy Gillespie's neat house looking out to the distant blue-green hills across the Border, his 12-year-old daughter made perfect sandwiches and tea for visitors. Her mother, Kathleen, trembled uncontrollably and told me how the child was alone in the house when the masked men came for her father.

It wasn't the first time death had come looking for Patsy Gillespie. Still disbelieving, his widow said: "I said to them 'You can't be coming for us a second time. Why?' We talked about his leaving Fort George after they made him drive a bomb there in 1986, but this is Derry and a job is a job. The details of her own story she told as though they had happened to somebody else. She and her children sat in the house until about 4 am, when the phone rang and one of the men in masking scarves ripped it out. After they had gone, she waited, then walked down the road by herself hoping to see her husband coming home. They had said he would be safe. Then she saw a neighbour's light was on and knocked on the door asking them to ring the local priest, anyone who might be able to find out what had happened.

Even in a community which did not any longer believe it could be shocked by violent death, what happened in Coshquin a week ago has stunned people.

A community leader in the Bogside, a man who makes no secret of his desire to see the British leave Northern Ireland, said to me: "If – and we still don't know if this is so – if the Provos did take a member of this community and force him to drive a bomb so that he himself died, then that is the worst thing that has happened here in the past 20 years."

Most people do not give the Provos the benefit of the doubt. In the *Derry Journal*, the editorial is headlined "Bloody Wednesday" and compares anger in the city to the reaction that followed Bloody Sunday in 1972. It reads: "No Irish nationalist forgets British guilt for centuries of oppression in this country, nor relieves Britain of a share of responsibility for what happens at present. But let no specious arguments about Britain's perfidy obscure the magnitude of the evil of the Coshquin bombing."

But in spite of this anger, reiterated in Bishop Edward Daly's sermon at Patsy Gillespie's funeral, nobody dares to hope that comments like these will change things or halt the accelerating pace of almost unbelievable events. A Sinn Féin councillor said to me: "Yes, it is very shocking, but people will absorb it. In a way that's the most depressing thing. By next week, most people will be more concerned about how Derry City will do in its next match. You must not forget that even now the security forces will be raiding houses and telling small boys that their fathers are murdering bastards. The pattern is set. We won't lose our own people."

IRA brings anarchy one stop nearer

What is new in Derry is a fear that attitudes have hardened to an extent that almost any atrocity can now be justified. That and a sense of isolation, abandonment almost, as far as the South is concerned.

Over and over again on Thursday and Friday, people said to me: "Did you see the RTÉ news? At least the BBC seemed to think that what had happened here was important." There was incredulity and considerable bitterness that RTÉ could devote almost all of its news bulletins to the Lenihan affair and that the human proxy bombs in the North, a terrifying escalation in the IRA's methods, warranted so little attention.

I cannot recall a time when the two parts of the country have seemed so separate, each indifferent to what is happening to the other. Perhaps that shouldn't matter, except that what happens on each side of the Border does, at least in the long term, affect the well-being of the other. Today's vote of confidence in the Dáil, the possibility of a general election, what happens in the politics of the Republic in the next few weeks has immediate implications for those people living in Coshquin and for their hopes of a more normal life.

For some time now, the British have been making it clear that they regard one of the most important factors affecting the Brooke initiative to be pressure of time. Up to now, what they have been talking about has been the possibility of a British general election and the fact that once this is seriously on the cards government ministers will have little inclination to consider new political moves in Northern Ireland. Now there is another much more pressing factor to deter them – the prospect of political instability down here. If British ministers become too preoccupied to worry overmuch about the North during the run-up to an election, experience has shown that this applies, only much more so, to the Republic.

Meanwhile, the North continues to pick itself up, to fix doors and windows, absorb what has happened as best it can.

Outside its immediate borders, very few people understand, or seem to care about, the moments like last Wednesday, when the screw is tightened another irreversible notch, bringing anarchy that bit closer. That is a matter for which we may, sooner or later, have to pay.

1991

An emotional attachment to the UN

JANUARY 23, 1991

"T is dangerous to take a cold, to sleep, to drink: but I tell you, my lord fool, out of this nettle, danger, we pluck this flower, safety." The Taoiseach's choice of a quote from Hotspur with which to end his speech to the Dáil in last Friday's debate was not entirely reassuring.

In *Henry IV, Part I*, poor Hotspur with his flaring notions of personal honour ends up very dead. In this most intensely political of Shakespeare's plays it is Prince Hal who demonstrates that he has the makings of a king, who knows that force of arms has its place but so, too, does the craft of politics which involves forging alliances with sometimes distasteful partners. In time, these skills would make him, according to Shakespeare, a great national leader imposing peace and stability at home and extending British interests abroad.

Perhaps after all, we should not worry quite so much about the way in which television bombards us with propaganda from the war zone. In 1945, *Henry V*, filmed in Wicklow with Irish archers, was still working well as a vehicle for patriotic emotions.

But back to our own concerns. The debate in the Dáil was late and necessary. It gave our representatives space to articulate deeply felt emotions at a time of crisis. In the manner of such events, it generated a great deal more heat than light. Mr Haughey's speech was masterly in its ambiguity. By the time he finished, it was still not absolutely clear whether he would endorse the refuelling of US planes at Shannon in the future.

We learned little about the present state of Irish neutrality, let alone its future. Instead, there was a great deal of quite understandable moral indignation from both sides on the Gulf conflict. We will hear a lot more of the same before peace returns to the Middle East.

Sickening stories of inhumanity are traded live on screen and there seems little to choose between them. Saddam Hussein's display of bruised and beaten prisoners of war confirms what we know of his terrifying record in dealing with his own people. Then, almost by chance, one reads a report that gas masks have been issued to Israelis living in the occupied territories, but not to Palestinians.

At times, the propaganda war waged by satellite seems to come down to a question of statistics, just how many bodies will opinion in the world at large be able to stand seeing on television? We have heard nothing of casualties in Iraq and are endlessly assured that the bombing has been surgical in its precision.

A leading British defence analyst has said that the number of civilians killed and maimed may be low, but that military casualties on the Iraqi side could well exceed 100,000. Almost as a footnote, another expert remarks that there is no way Iraq will be able to deal with this. For a country of 17 million people, there are 250 hospital beds for serious burn cases and a further 300 beds for emergencies. What this will mean for the peace process in the Middle East is not yet a matter for speculation.

The main emphasis in the Dáil debate, from the

Government and the Fine Gael benches, was in our commitment to meeting our responsibilities as a member of the UN.
This is almost certainly in tune with public opinion in the
country as a whole – for the moment. Although writers to the
letters column of this paper have voiced strong opposition to
the war, this has not been translated into larger numbers of
people attending demonstrations or prayer meetings in the
streets or in churches.

I am told that, per capita, protests in this country have been
the smallest in Europe and that far fewer people have been
moved to demonstrate than came out during Ronald Reagan's
visit, to protest against US policy in Latin America.

Why? Those who have been involved in trying to mobilise
opposition to the Gulf conflict say that two reasons come up
again and again. One is the strength of feeling – approaching
racism in some cases – not only against Saddam Hussein but
against the Arab world in general. This seems curious in view
of Ireland's extremely sympathetic stance on the Palestinians
but may have to do with the media coverage of Islamic
fundamentalism, oil-rich sheiks, undemocratic regimes.

The other, much more powerful, reason cited for approval
of action in the Gulf is emotional support for the United
Nations. Very many people seem to define Ireland's place in
the world through our membership of the UN, which is seen
as being in some way more idealistic than belonging to the
European Community.

They take quite justifiable pride in the activities of Irish
soldiers deployed in the UN peacekeeping forces over the
years. The UN is perceived as having given us an international
voice independent of Britain and respected abroad, and its
work is thought of as, in some ways, similar to that of Irish
missionaries.

But if the present military alliance in the Gulf demonstrates
anything, it is that the credibility of the UN as an independent

force in world affairs now faces a desperate challenge. Nobody who watches the nightly coverage on television can take seriously the claim made (when they remember) by American and British politicians that the military might now deployed in the Gulf constitutes a UN force.

Colonel E D Doyle, writing in this paper, put it succinctly: "It is a force authorised to take action by a UN resolution but it is certainly not a UN force. Its commander, General Norman Schwartzkopf, need not report to the Security Council, nor does it fight under a UN flag."

A worrying number of international legal experts have argued that, under pressure of world events, the United Nations has been virtually transformed into an instrument of the United States, and its resolutions used to give the cover of legitimacy to American foreign policy decisions. Many people, certainly many Americans, would argue that there was no alternative to this. The ending of the Cold War between the superpowers, the crisis within the Soviet Union, made it a matter of the utmost urgency to impose what President Bush himself has described as a "new world order where the rule of law, not the law of the jungle, governs the conduct of nations."

The United States, they say, is the only country with resources and the necessary political will to do the job. But *Pax Americana* is a very long way from the original ideal of an even-handed system of collective security enshrined in the UN Charter, to which Ireland has loyally subscribed and for which Irish soldiers have died.

Pax Americana, like *Pax Brittanica* before it, is highly selective. Noam Chomsky, himself a vehement critic of Saddam Hussein, has detailed the number of occasions on which the United States, followed closely by Britain, has vetoed attempts by the Security Council to resist, by collective UN action, aggression against member states.

Another point has been made about the nature of the military coalition at present operating in the Gulf, which should concern us. In hard political terms, the most immediate obvious result of the conflict is that it has breathed new life into the Anglo-American alliance, which had seemed virtually moribund. Certainly, British commentators believe that the main benefit for their country is that it strengthens the anti-European lobby in the UK and puts on the long finger any move towards a closer political union with the EC.

The initial reaction to this view in Dublin has been that this could benefit us too, that the whole debate about Irish neutrality within the European context may now be postponed. But this will present us with difficult choices. As far as the Gulf War and its eventual resolution is concerned, we may well find ourselves much closer to the views of the French, the Germans, even little Luxembourg, whose last-minute offers of a peace initiative have been so comprehensively derided by the British media. Like them, we have urged that any peace conference be linked to finding a solution to the Palestinian problem, a hope which recedes as America's fortunes in the Gulf become more dependent on Israel.

It is early days yet and this is a debate which has hardly started. There is a danger that in the weeks ahead it will be clouded, not only by the barrage of conflicting stories from the Gulf but by our own historic attachments. I am tempted to end with a quote from the end of *Henry IV, Part II,* but leave that to Mr Haughey.

Wrong time to keep out Sinn Féin

Next Monday, unless the Labour Party decides to withdraw its motion, it seems virtually certain that Dublin City Council will vote to stop Sinn Féin holding its ard-fheis next February in the Mansion House.

The arguments against allowing Sinn Féin the use of a public building in the centre of the capital are familiar and can be summed up in the pithy phrase: "Murder in the Mansion House". They are persuasive to many people who find it deeply offensive that an organisation which they see as a propaganda front for the IRA should be allowed to conduct itself in public just like any other political party.

Already my heart sinks as I start to write this column. I know that it will offend some readers, provoke angry letters and draw down on me the accusation that I am ambivalent about the IRA's terrorist campaign. Nonetheless, it seems important to put forward the case – and maybe even persuade some people to think about the issue – why I believe the proposed ban constitutes an unnecessary and dangerous extension of political censorship and, as important, that it will do nothing to help bring an end to the tragic violence in the North. Not to do so would be to bow to a particularly insidious form of censorship – that which we journalists too often impose on ourselves.

The arguments against this ban fall into two categories. The first is rooted squarely in a liberal defence of freedom of expression. It may be that in some situations, when the security of the State or its citizens are under threat, it does become necessary to curtail the public expression of political views. We are not in that situation, nor is there any reason to suppose that we are close to it. That is why the Labour Party has been consistently opposed to Section 31 of the Broadcasting Act.

Much of the time during a Sinn Féin ard-fheis is taken up, as with any other political party, in arguing about standing orders and debates on bread-and-butter issues.

Some of the views expressed, particularly those which relate to the violence in Northern Ireland, are scandalous to many people in Dublin. But like it or not, they form part of the ongoing political debate about the future of their country. To attempt to censor them from the public platform, as they have already been censored from RTÉ, constitutes a further erosion of the right to free speech, which is one of the hallmarks of a mature democracy.

To say that the Provisional IRA cares nothing for liberal values and that its idea of political debate all too often takes the form of a bullet in the head, is to miss the point. If there is one thing that the past 20 years of violence should have taught us, it is that the erosion of any individual civil rights represents a threat to all of us.

But there is another, perhaps even more pressing reason why those involved in putting forward the motion calling for a ban on Sinn Féin should reconsider their positions. To keep the Provos out of the Mansion House may be a cause of satisfaction to those citizens who view the violence in the North with horror and do not want to be reminded of it, least of all in the centre of Dublin. There is no reason to suppose that the ban will have any benign effect on the IRA. On the contrary, the evidence from Northern Ireland where, over the years, a whole catalogue of restrictions has been introduced to limit political activity, is that these damage and weaken Sinn Féin but inflict no real damage on the IRA.

If anything, the effect has been to undermine those within the republican movement who are prepared to argue for political methods by furnishing more young people, cynical about politics as an effective method of achieving change, into the IRA.

At the moment, the most important challenge facing anyone who wants to help end the killing in the North is to try to persuade the Provos to call off their campaign. If this were to happen, it would transform the prospects for an equitable settlement. But it will only happen, as Peter Brooke was brave enough to admit publicly, when those within the "terrorist community" decide that the time has come to end the violence and to pursue their objectives by political means. It is a sad irony that, according to a recent opinion poll on Channel 4 television, very many people in Britain now recognise that at the end of the day there will be a lasting peace only when Sinn Féin is brought into the political process. There remains a precondition, for the forseeable future at least, that the IRA should call off the violence.

It will be said that nobody is trying to stop the Provos from holding their ard-fheis, that there is nothing to prevent them from hiring a conference room at a large hotel or one of the trade union halls around Dublin at which meetings are regularly held. The aim of next week's vote in the City Council is to keep them out of the Mansion House, which is not just a large public building in the city centre but one redolent with hallowed historical associations. That, of course, is why the Provos want to go on holding their ard-fheis there.

In recent weeks and months, as the sickening pattern of tit-for-tat killings has threatened to spiral out of control, the hope that any debate about strategy is going on without the Provisional movement has become hard to sustain. It may be that it will be possible to revive it during the forthcoming ard-fheis.

It is not a good time for Dublin City Council to make life more difficult for those within Sinn Féin who continue to make the case for politics, the long hard slog of the ballot paper over the Armalite.

1992

A woman's right to speak denied

FEBRUARY 19, 1992

"May I have one minute of this House's time on behalf of the women in Ireland?" Monica Barnes, her voice tense with emotion, appealed to the Ceann Comhairle to be allowed to speak during the time allotted to the Dáil to discuss the case of the 14-year-old who has been prohibited from going to England for an abortion.

No. Out of order. Please, can we have a little respect for the rules of the House?

If ever there was a metaphor for a society in which men control the structures of power and are determined to keep it that way, it was the Dáil yesterday afternoon. There were nine women deputies in the chamber and row upon row of middle-aged men in suits.

It had been agreed that four of these men, all party leaders, would speak for 10 minutes each on the case of the girl pregnant as a result of rape. Why not? It was a man who raped her, a man who put her into court, a man who handed down judgment on her future.

One by one, the four women on the Fine Gael benches rose and, with varying degrees of the humility proper to their sex, begged the man in charge of proceedings to be allowed to speak. "I am only an ordinary deputy," Nuala Fennell began, "but I am a woman". By the time we got to Madeleine

Taylor-Quinn, there was a bit more aggression visible. "This isn't a point of order," the Chair reproached her. "No, it's a protest," she snapped back.

It would be nice to report that the Minister of State with responsibility for, among other things, Women's Affairs, stood up for these women's right to speak. Tom Kitt was there but remained silent. He does not look like a man who is going to challenge anybody's house rules on behalf of the women in Ireland.

Earlier, the party leaders, starting with the Taoiseach, had said their pieces. They were sympathetic, concerned, above all reasonable. Mr Reynolds put on record the House's sympathy for those concerned in "this most distressful case". Dick Spring gave a masterly exposition of the legal background to the judgment and the nightmarish implications for the future. Proinsias De Rossa came a bit closer to the kind of emotion that women feel about this case when he said: "How many TDs in this House who are parents of young girls could put their hands on their hearts and say that they would not have taken the same course as the parents of this child?" Albert Reynolds looked up. It was a week to the day since he was elected Taoiseach. Last Tuesday, his daughters, bright as butterflies and pretty as paint, brought a warm glow to the Dáil with their evident pride in their father's achievement.

The men responsible for the constitutional amendment were there yesterday: Garret FitzGerald, listening intently, Charles Haughey, hunched in the seat in the back row. The most intriguing sight in the Dáil, at least for this observer, was the conversation between the former Fianna Fáil leader and the new Minister for Justice. Mr Haughey had invited Pádraig Flynn to sit down beside him and was talking fast and emphatically, jabbing his finger in the air. At one point, he looked at the Minister for Justice and clapped the palm of his hand to his forehead in a gesture of (dare one say it?) Shakespearean despair.

Mr Haughey, like all but one of the women in the Dáil, is now an ordinary backbench deputy and so we were not allowed to hear what he might have wanted to say about the constitutional amendment and its application through the courts. Pity.

This week, at least 100 women will travel to England for abortions. It will be an even more desolate journey than usual because of what has happened in recent days. It is shameful, but not, alas, surprising that no woman was allowed to speak for them in what a former Taoiseach once described as "the democratic forum of the nation".

Why a "Yes" vote can further the interests of Irish women

JUNE 11, 1992

It may be some comfort to Irish women who are still worried about the threat to their rights implicit in Protocol 17, and not entirely reassured by the statement issued earlier this week by the four party leaders, to know that information about abortion facilities in Britain is now available at the Government Publications Shop in Dublin's Molesworth Street. For £1.50 you can buy the Official Report of the Dáil proceedings for May 21st. This contains, on page 159, Proinsias De Rossa's speech on the seizure earlier that day of the *Guardian* newspaper, in which he quoted an extract from the offending advertisement for the Marie Stopes Clinic, including telephone numbers of several of its branches in London. Or then again, you may see it as just another example of the uncertainty and double-think which now characterise so much of the debate on Maastricht and matters relating to it. We are in some state of confusion, if not of actual chaos.

Given that the whole legal basis of the treaty has been thrown open to doubt by the result of the Danish poll, one hears more and more people who seem to regard our own referendum as an opportunity for what Erica Jong might describe as a zipless protest: no awkward fumblings at the start, no worries about the consequences afterwards. They see it as a chance to send a message to the Brussels fat cats, to the Government, even to the media, about a whole range of issues ranging from the Irish soul, through women's rights, to unemployment and the depopulation of the West. But what kind of message will a "No" vote send, and to whom?

Last week, just after the Danish rejection of Maastricht had thrown politicians across Europe into disarray, I went to a meeting of women TDs drawn from all the parties in the Oireachtas, at which Nuala Fennell was speaking. She talked with angry eloquence of the impotence and frustration she had experienced in trying to focus the attention of male colleagues on the sense of outrage which very many women feel about the Maastricht debate and, in particular the threat to their rights implicit in the protocol.

On that very day, once again, reaction in the Dáil to an important development, i.e. the Danish poll and the possibility it raised that the treaty would have to be renegotiated, was confined to the male leaders of the political parties. No woman deputy was allowed to speak. She had found, when talking to male deputies, that the various women's organisations and campaign groups expressing these concerns were, quite simply, "invisible". There were some honourable exceptions to this general rule but they were very few. Most TDs, when they look at opposition to Maastricht, in their own constituencies or waiting outside the Dáil, see the ranks of what "one might loosely describe" as Family Solidarity Inc. Yes, they know that some people are worried about neutrality and matters of that ilk, but that kind of opposition does not pose the kind of political threat that could become seriously worrying in an election. Other speakers at the meeting made the point that a large "No" vote, particularly if it led to a rejection of the Maastricht Treaty, would be claimed as a victory by Senator Des Hanafin and his supporters, and would certainly be seen as such by most professional politicians.

This was brought home to me, even more forcibly, by a senior member of Fianna Fáil whom I met, quite by chance, at the weekend. He had come to a hotel in the midlands for an internal meeting of the party to discuss how best to launch and run the Maastricht campaign locally. On this particular evening, there was some concern that "Pro-Life" supporters within the party would disrupt the meeting in protest against the Government's decision to go ahead with the Maastricht referendum without first publishing the wording of a new amendment on abortion. This man is politically robust, well able to see off the kind of pressure associated with telephone calls from members of SPUC. For him, like many TDs in rural constituencies, what is far more worrying is the fact that some of the most ardent members of the anti-abortion lobby in his own constituency are also the hardest workers, in good times and bad, for Fianna Fáil. He will need them when the election comes around and does not want to alienate them now.

Since the Danish poll, we have been told over and over again by our political leaders, that the referendum next week is a chance for us to demonstrate that our commitment to the European ideal amounts to more than holding out a bottom-less begging bowl. But the vote next Thursday will also send – and it may be just as important – a significant message to Albert Reynolds and his ministers, particularly when the results in individual constituencies are broken down and analysed.

When he became Taoiseach, Mr Reynolds spoke of his desire to be remembered as the Irish leader who opened the shutters and let the light shine in. To date we haven't seen much evidence of this but, to be fair, it hasn't been very good political weather for throwing open the windows to great gusts of fresh air. Nor is there much reason to believe that the climate is going to improve. On the contrary, most politicians to whom I've spoken, particularly in Fianna Fáil, think that the Maastricht campaign is only the beginning and that the going will get "really bumpy" come the autumn, when they have to face at least one referendum on abortion and issues relating to it. There is no reason, as yet, to cast doubts on Mr Reynolds's sincerity when he talks of letting in the light. His speech to his party's ard-fheis reiterated his desire to preside over a more tolerant and compassionate society in Ireland. But he is also a Fianna Fáil leader with his mind firmly fixed on the need to achieve an overall majority for his party in a general election, and that is what will determine the political course he decides to steer once the Maastricht referendum is out of the way. Inevitably, he will be much influenced by the results of next week's poll, particularly when it comes to how he and his party approach the social agenda. We already know that there are a number of items on that agenda which are likely to provoke strong opposition from Family Solidarity and its supporters within Fianna Fáil. Not just the truly daunting prospect of a referendum followed by legislation on abortion, but also divorce, the decriminalising of homosexuality, the wider availability of condoms, proper education on AIDS. And so on, and on, and on.

It has become fashionable, particularly in the context of the current debate, to dismiss these issues as part of an alien "liberal" agenda, using the word "liberal" as a synonym for "un-Irish". Unhappily, nothing could be further from the truth. Anyone who writes about these subjects, and receives desperately unhappy letters and phone calls about them, knows that they are as Irish as bacon and cabbage and that the misery resulting from them is not confined to Dublin 4. On the contrary, for a young girl who finds herself unhappily pregnant, or a gay man who cannot "come out" for fear of the pain this might cause to his parents, or a helpless wife trapped in a violent marriage, the chances of having access to the kind of information, counselling and support needed to rebuild a life become more remote the further he or she lives from relatively easygoing Dublin.

Like very many women who have felt patronised by male political leaders lecturing me on my economic responsibilities and infuriated by their refusal to take women's concerns about the protocol seriously, I have felt tempted by the result of the Danish poll to succumb to the giddy delights of voting "No". After all, if the treaty will almost certainly have to be renegotiated anyway, why not register a protest? Here's why. First, I agree with the Council for the Status of Women that very many of the social reforms we have achieved in this country would never have happened without the European Community.

Mary Robinson's record, the very fact of her Presidency, bears potent witness to that. But even more, in the present context of uncertainty regarding the treaty itself, the result of next week's poll will be extremely important in the domestic political context. I want to ensure that every chance is given to Albert Reynolds to make good the pledges he gave to us when he was elected leader of Fianna Fáil, about opening the shutters and letting in the light. Even if his Government wins this referendum, facing up to that challenge will still be daunting. If there is a "No" vote, which will be interpreted as a victory for the most reactionary forces in Irish society, the process will be (dare I say it?) aborted before we have a chance even to glimpse the sun.

There are many other extremely important strands to the Maastricht debate but this, I believe, is how I can best try to ensure that my vote helps towards creating the kind of society I want to see in Ireland for the children I brought home to live in this country.

Disenfranchised resentful at exclusion from change

DECEMBER 3, 1992

Dan Sweeney, who owns the Mad Hatter bar on New York's Second Avenue and 77th Street, has good things to say about Dick Spring. "Even when he was waiting on tables here he was a consummate diplomat. We would be delighted to see him back, but I gather he's gone on to greater things. He came to us through sport originally. As you see, we have strong sporting connections." The bar is festooned with American football helmets and other memorabilia. An Irish barman remembers the Labour Party leader as "a lovely hurler. I saw him play at Gaelic Park in the Bronx. He might not find it so easy to get a game now because there are many more teams".

In one corner of the bar, a group of emigrants has a different interest in the fortunes of Dick Spring. Despite the recession and the fall in emigration at home, there are still large numbers of young Irish people visible in New York. Talking to some of them earlier this week, I found them intensely interested in the general election and resentful that they had not been able to vote in it. Most had read Irish newspaper coverage of the campaign and talked to relatives at home about the prospects for candidates in their own constituencies. As well as this, and perhaps a sign of changing political attitudes among the new emigrants, the *Irish Voice* newspaper in New York has carried detailed reports and editorials on the subject throughout the campaign.

The possibility of a strong Labour input to a new government has raised the hopes of those who have been campaigning in Britain and Australia as well as the US for the franchise to be extended to emigrants. The arguments for and against the proposal have been well rehearsed in this paper, but with a general election just behind us, it is perhaps timely to recap on a little recent history.

Last year, the Labour Party introduced a Private Member's Bill proposing that anyone who had left Ireland within the past 15 years should be allowed to vote in the constituency in which he or she had last resided. The Bill was opposed by the then government and defeated in spite of the fact that the Programme for Government contained a commitment to examine proposals for extending the franchise to emigrants.

If it had been passed, the Labour Party proposal would have brought Ireland into line with other EC countries as well as the US, Canada and the newly emerging states of eastern Europe. The objection to Labour's proposals appears to focus on two points. The first, which has also been made in letters written to this paper, is that there should be "no representation without taxation". To this the would-be voters in the emigrant community reply that nobody has ever suggested that paying taxes should be a qualification for voting, otherwise it would be necessary to disenfranchise large sections of the resident population, including the unemployed, students, and so on. More insidious is the argument, which I have heard voiced privately by politicians, that under the PR system, where the transfer of preferences is often crucial to getting a candidate elected, it would be very difficult to target and "manage" the emigrant vote. "In other words," as one emigrant said to me with some, annoyance, "they don't want us to have the vote because we might influence the result in a way they couldn't control."

Talking to members of the Irish Emigrant Vote Campaign in New York this week, the most striking thing was how much they wanted to emphasise that extending the franchise should be seen as a positive thing not just for those who would get to vote but for the country they have left. David O'Leary, a lawyer who came to New York seven years ago, said Ireland lost the 1950s generation of emigrants. "We don't want that to happen this time around. All the recent reports on the economy take it for granted that emigration is going to continue, at least until the year 2000. The State has made an enormous investment in those who leave. They are well educated and resourceful. "Many of them would be glad to repay some of that investment. By giving emigrants the vote, the government would demonstrate that it wants a constructive engagement with Irish people who have left but who still feel involved in what is happening at home." Another member of the group made the point that the Government's economic policy, particularly its proposals for job-creation, will directly affect what happens to young emigrants; yet their voice is never heard when such policies are being debated.

These are issues which seem to be more important to them than the more usual ones of funding for emigrant groups and so on. The campaign is ambivalent about Fine Gael's proposal that the way to give emigrants a voice is to allocate special seats in the Seanad for the emigrant community. On the one hand, its members welcome the fact that Fine Gael has taken the issue seriously and recognises the importance of the principle involved. On the other hand, they argue that the effect of having special Seanad seats would be to marginalise the whole issue of emigration.

What is needed, they say, is for emigrants to be able to exercise the kind of political clout that comes from voting for candidates in Dáil elections. Most of all they want it accepted that many emigrants, particularly the young who have left in recent years, hope to return to Ireland; that they have every right to be concerned about what is happening at home and should be allowed to express that concern through the ballot box. To date, only the Labour Party has seemed to accept this argument fully. But most other parties, including at various times individual members of Fianna Fail, have agreed that the emigrants have a case.

There is another reason, just now, why politicians engaged in negotiating the shape of a new government should consider the issue. In all the acres of newsprint devoted to analysing the general election, everybody has agreed on one thing. The electorate voted for change, not just in terms of new policies, but for a different way of conducting the government of the State. We all know that, given the present state of the economy, it will be extremely difficult for any new administration, whatever its composition, to make policy changes – even in areas like job-creation – which involve big increases in public spending. But it should be possible to signal a commitment to a different style which would take account of the electorate's desire for a more open system, giving people more access to the process of decision-making rather than excluding them.

Extending the franchise to the hundreds of thousands of young people who have had to leave Ireland to seek work and who will leave in the years ahead is an obvious item for this agenda. It would give real substance to the symbolic light which President Robinson placed in the window of Áras an Uachtaráin, by bringing our emigrants back into the political community.

Afraid to be identified

Imagine being invited to Áras an Uachtaráin by the President, Mrs Robinson, being frightened that your parents might hear about it or that your neighbours might see you on TV.

For some members of the gay and lesbian community, who were made welcome by Mrs Robinson last Saturday morning, this was a sad but inescapable element of their visit. Before going to the Park, at breakfast in a nearby hotel, they were asked if they were willing to be interviewed or filmed with the President.

About half of the 34 people said that they did not want, could not afford, to be identified. What a reproach to the rest of us. That guests of the President should feel that they had to conceal a meeting which, for the overwhelming majority of people in Ireland, would be something to talk about with pride.

When Mrs Robinson arrived to greet the group, one young woman ducked behind me as the cameras followed the President and her husband around the room. It would, she said, be "disastrous" if she was seen on the RTÉ news. Yes, she was active in a local group, but her employer did not know she was a lesbian.

Some, who had come from north of the Border, had other

worries. A young man in a dark suit told me that his neighbours in east Belfast knew he was gay, and there was no problem with that, but he was not at all sure that they would take kindly to his shaking hands with the President of the Republic.

For everybody present in the beautiful drawing room, the occasion was an enormously important and positive experience, personally as well as politically. You could have cut the emotional atmosphere with a knife.

Some of those present were close to tears, particularly when Mrs Robinson talked to members of Parents' Enquiry, mothers and fathers of gay people who counsel others trying to understand and come to terms with their children's sexuality.

Representatives of groups from six different cities each said a few words. Over and over again, from both sides of the Border and in both official languages, the same point was made. Now that you, Mrs Robinson, have made us welcome in your home, the gay and lesbian community may begin to feel itself brought in from the margins of Irish society.

What was left unsaid, although the message came through clear as a bell, was that now perhaps, after this, a new government will be shamed into changing the laws on homosexuality. It is more than four years since the European Court of Human Rights found in favour of David Norris and the Government first promised to implement its decision.

Unless a Bill is brought forward early in the new year, this State will be called upon to explain, once again, to the Court of Human Rights in Strasbourg why it has failed to act.

Rereading the shameful catalogue of excuses and prevarication, it seems that successive governments have seen no real need to change the laws at all, let alone to do so as a matter of urgency.

After all, the politicians reply when asked directly, gay

people are neither prosecuted nor harassed in Ireland. For heaven's sake, the only public figure who has declared himself to be homosexual is a well-liked and respected member of the Seanad.

Why stir up all the inevitable opposition from the usual quarters when there is so much else that needs to be tackled in the field of social reform?

The gay community, quite understandably, does not see it that way. Jeff Dudgeon, whose case at Strasbourg against the British government forced through a change in the laws in Northern Ireland, is convinced that it was this which paved the way for a shift in social attitudes in that part of the island. The law, as we are often told, is a great persuader.

Dan Donnelly, who wrote to the President originally to ask for a meeting on behalf of gay groups in Limerick, agrees. A change in the law is absolutely necessary, not only to remove the stigma of criminality and all the fears that spring from it, but also to make it possible to have a proper campaign against discrimination in housing and employment.

Although this has been outlawed in the public service, it still exists in the private sector and is almost impossible to combat under the present laws.

Others cite the fact that financial support has been consistently denied to gay groups, even when the work that these are doing, in the field of AIDS for example, has been recognised as important by individual ministers. There are other day-to-day instances of discrimination which again are almost impossible to resist – newspapers which have refused to take advertisements from gay groups, hotels which do not allow them to book public rooms, pubs where new management suddenly refuses them service.

All this is, or should be, immediately relevant to the present talks about the formation of a new government, particularly if this is to take the form of a Fianna Fáil/Labour Party coalition.

Since the general election, the phrase "the people voted for change" has been repeated like a mantra from early morning to late at night by every politician with access to the airwaves. But much of the change that people want, in terms of creating more jobs, building more houses, putting more money into the health services, will depend on the economy and, anyway, will take time to achieve.

There is one way in which Labour, as partner in a new coalition, can demonstrate its commitment to quite fundamental change and to progress towards a more tolerant and inclusive society. That is to insist on the inclusion, in any agreed programme for government, of a firm timetable for the introduction of those reforms from which its predecessors, particularly in Fianna Fáil, have run away, including changing the laws on homosexuality.

Not for the first time, our President, effortlessly and generously subversive of entrenched prejudice, has given a signal that cannot he ignored.

1993

Bewilderment over society's failure to provide protection

MARCH 11, 1993

"It seems that we are fated to mark out our progress in terms of cases – the X case, the Kerry Babies case, now the Kilkenny case."

Mary Dorcey was speaking at the Abbey Theatre last Sunday night, introducing a poem from her marvellous collection, *Moving into the Space Created by Our Mothers*.

The evening had been organised to mark International Women's Day and included 12 poets from Ireland and Europe reading from their works. The President, Mrs Robinson, radiantly welcoming, said that last year's celebration had left her "on a high", but last Sunday, the mood was more sombre and inevitably overshadowed by the harrowing revelations of the previous weeks.

Mrs Robinson – who, in a previous life, saw so much of the often brutal reality of many women's lives as cases in the courts – responded to the audience's sense of bewilderment. It seemed to her "appropriate, highly appropriate" that the practical aim of the evening was to raise money for Women's Aid, the organisation which tries against financial odds to provide refuge for women who have been battered, and who almost always have nowhere else to turn.

What has been almost impossible for most of us to comprehend about this latest case is that the young woman in Kilkenny did ask for help, insofar as it was in her power to do so, and that the practical support which she and her mother needed was not forthcoming, at least not until one garda took upon herself the responsibility which society collectively had evaded for 16 years.

And yet, to those who have experience in dealing firsthand with the victims of this kind of violence (for example in battered wives' refuges) it came as no surprise at all that the various agencies involved – gardaí, social services and, most of all perhaps, the medical profession – failed this young woman.

Breaking the Silence: a report on violence in the home, produced last year by the policy research centre for the Mid-Western Health Board and the ADAPT refuge in Limerick, explains in great detail that it is not just in Ireland that the police, social workers and doctors consistently avoid confronting the real issue of violence within the home, even with evidence of it presented to them in the most stark terms.

Since the Minister for Health, Mr Howlin, set up an inquiry to investigate the Kilkenny case, we have heard appeals that there should be no "scapegoats", and that Ms Catherine McGuinness SC and her team must take full account of the practical dilemma which faced those in the caring professions who came in contact with the Kilkenny woman.

Already a sub-text has emerged that somehow this family was different, set apart from the rest of the community by being members of a different religion from the majority – as though this not only helps to explain why the father brutalised his wife and daughter but also goes some way to excuse this society's failure to protect them.

We have heard these weasel words before. They are used in the North, not exactly to condone murder but to explain away why individuals are killed – because a nephew was a Sinn Féin councillor, or an uncle was in the RUC.

We have been urged to look at ourselves, at the nature of Irish society, the influence of the Catholic Church in making individuals and the social agencies of the State reluctant to interfere in what is seen as the privacy of the family, particularly the nuclear family. And of course, it is right that we should do these things, since it is only by learning more about ourselves that we will be able to understand why these cases continue to explode onto the news pages, horrifying us each time they happen.

But equally, it is important to remember that as a society we do set up structures, employing people who are supposedly trained to recognise the alarm signals and set in train the procedures, legal and medical, to protect the most weak and vulnerable, who are almost always women and children.

The woman at the centre of this case, accompanied quite often by her terrified mother, did attempt, while under the threat of further violence, to engage the active interest of the police, the medical profession and social workers. They may have tried to help but given what they knew or suspected was happening to her, their responses were – to put it mildly – desperately inadequate.

Two gardaí summoned to the house asked her in front of her father, who had just beaten her, if she wanted to make a statement. When she refused, they left. Even so, they showed themselves to be more concerned than many of their colleagues who refuse to answer calls to deal with complaints of domestic violence on the grounds that it is not "serious police work".

The response of a doctor sought out by the mother and daughter to help them was, according to the victim, to invite the father to his surgery to discuss the problem. The man walked out. We are not told what happened to his wife and daughter when they returned home.

Research in other countries indicates that medical and nursing staff in the casualty departments of large hospitals can be crucial in recognising the signs of domestic injuries and persuading the victim, in an environment where she feels relatively safe, to take the first steps to break the cycle of violence. In the end, that is what happened in this case, but we need to know why it did not happen on the other occasions when this young woman arrived in hospital with serious injuries.

Ms McGuinness will have to discover why it was that Garda Agnes Reddy was able to break through all the legal and social obstacles to succeed in saving this young woman where so many others had failed. What was different about her training, attitudes, commitment, from those of the doctors, and social workers who had listened to the same story and presumably seen the same injuries?

She might start by asking the ethics committee of the Medical Council its view of the social and professional responsibilities of a doctor in caring for a patient who has been subjected to violent sexual assaults by a father.

We know, because their representatives told us last week, that gardaí and professional social workers feel a sense of anguish about this case and the failure to bring the victim's ordeal to an end much sooner. We have yet to hear from any organisation representing the medical profession (who are not slow to give us the benefit of their views on abortion and other issues) any word of explanation or regret for what happened to this most vulnerable patient.

Courage to back an unpopular cause may light the way ahead

MARCH 25, 1993

THE PAST week has presented us with a poignant contrast between two communities of the Irish diaspora. In Washington, there was the glad, confident morning of St Patrick's Day; Irish-Americans enjoying their success as a group wielding the kind of political clout that enabled them to make demands on the most powerful leader in the most powerful country in the world.

As President Clinton led the singing of 'When Irish Eyes are Smiling', men with such names as Kennedy, Feley, Gallagher and Coyle grinned in dazzling approbation. It was impossible not to think of those who had gone before, of the emigrant poor who had seized the opportunities offered by this new country and whose sons and daughters now moved with such ease and self-assurance that even the high kitsch of the St Patrick's Day ceremonies seemed a cause for legitimate celebration.

How tragically different from Warrington, where this week the children and grandchildren of other emigrants live in fear that their homes may be attacked, or they themselves abused when people hear that they have Irish accents.

In New York, I met a young Irishman, a construction

worker, who told me why he had come to the United States, even though in many ways he would have preferred to stay in England where he used to work.

He had lived in London for several years, buying his morning paper every day at the same corner shop before going to work. One morning, after there had been an IRA bomb in some English town, the owner, who had always been perfectly friendly, said to him in front of a queue of other customers that he would prefer if he did not come into the shop again. The young man went straight back to his digs, packed his case and went home to Ireland.

"I just couldn't bear to stay in that hostile atmosphere, feeling that people blamed me for what had happened," he said to me, and shuddered at the memory as we sat in a New York bar.

There must be people in Warrington this week who have come to know that feeling very well. There have been appeals for calm, and the local police have stressed, "The Irish community is very well respected here."

But any Irish person who has lived in Britain at a time when the IRA has been involved in placing bombs will recognise that moment of wondering whether English people – strangers, friends, colleagues – blame one for the deaths and injuries that have been suffered.

Is it better to try to explain, honestly enough, that most Irish people do not support this kind of activity? Or will that sound like a pathetic attempt to slither away from responsibility for acts which are, after all, rooted in the troubled history of our two countries?

For months now, ever since the IRA started its latest campaign in Britain, there has been foreboding that, sooner or later, there was going to be some dreadful tragedy, comparable with the Birmingham pub bombings of 1974. For most people who have watched the progress of events, while the

IRA has seemed to take increasingly dangerous risks, the miracle has been that there has not been a vicious reaction before now against the Irish living in Britain.

In part, at least as far as the authorities and the media are concerned, this has been due to the impact on British public opinion of such cases as the Birmingham Six and the Guildford Four. That such miscarriages of justice could happen as a result of the public's desire for vengeance served as a warning to a fundamentally decent people that the distinction must be drawn between the Irish community as a whole and those who had committed such atrocities.

The other reason that, so far, there has been no major backlash against the Irish community is that bombs in Britain do not yet have the same impact as in Northern Ireland, where a whole community feels itself attacked whenever an atrocity occurs.

Writing in this paper just a few weeks ago, when bombs went off in a busy shopping street in Camden Town, I said that Britain was simply too large, and British society too fragmented, for the IRA to achieve the kind of political effect it sought. For this to happen, it would need to inflict injuries on a scale which, at least until very recently, has been quite unacceptable to its own supporters.

It may be that this has now changed, that the IRA on the evidence of recent bombings is prepared to escalate its campaign in a new and horrifying way, in which case both governments will be facing a crisis much worse than anything that has happened in the past 23 years.

The reaction in this State to what happened last Saturday in Warrington has been horrified revulsion, accompanied by a rush of condemnation and a natural desire to explain that Irish people are appalled at seeing innocent children killed in their name. But, as more than one commentator has already remarked, if blanket condemnation was going to persuade the

IRA to change its tactics, the campaign of violence would have ended long ago.

Expressions of revulsion from politicians are not enough. If this violence, suffered by both communities in Northern Ireland as well as Britain, is to be brought to an end, it will be done only by politicians capable of taking serious and, to many people, repugnant risks.

In the recent past, we have had politicians, mainly British, who have been prepared to show this kind of courage in setting out the stark realities of the conflict – that the violence will end only when those who hold power within the 'terrorist community' are persuaded that their campaign is counter-productive, and that they should lay down their weapons and pursue their objectives by political means.

Nobody with any sense of politics believes this process will be either smooth or easy. There must now be real fears that a section of the IRA's leadership believes that an escalation of the campaign in Britain with yet more appalling casualties will affect public opinion in that country in such a way that it will lead to an irresistible demand for British withdrawal from Northern Ireland.

But equally, there are others, at least within Sinn Féin, who are clearly fearful of the scenario which could now be threatening in Britain, and who are actively seeking ways to bring about an honourable compromise that could lead to peace. They are also prepared to consider the argument that the continuing violence is driving the two communities in Northern Ireland farther apart and is, for that reason, politically counterproductive.

But for this debate to become a political reality, somebody, sooner or later, is going to have to initiate a process of meaningful dialogue with Sinn Féin. In the immediate aftermath of Warrington, this is not likely to be a popular cause.

And yet, even as the easy cries of condemnation have filled the air, some politicians have been brave enough to say that if we are serious in our desire for peace, then this is what we must do.

Gordon Wilson persists, despite the rebuffs he has received, in his determination to talk with the IRA. Séamus Mallon detects a change in the thinking of the Provisionals and urges the British Secretary of State to take this seriously and to meet it with a generous response. David Norris makes the point, on *Questions and Answers*, that violence is never all on one side and that it is often necessary for governments to talk to very unpleasant people in order to achieve peace.

These three men have all been forthright in their condemnation of paramilitary violence. But as well as this, they share a quality of moral courage which has meant, in the past, that none of them has shirked speaking out, even when the truth has been far from comfortable either for them or for their listeners.

In a week when there has been very little reason for hope, they just may have given us a beacon to light the way ahead.

Have they gone far enough for Sinn Féin to deliver the IRA?

DECEMBER 16, 1993

Yesterday morning, as journalists and television crews gathered in Downing Street for a scheduled photo call of John Major greeting Albert Reynolds, our attention was diverted by the sudden appearance of a figure in khaki battle fatigues and a chequered head dress. Yasser Arafat was visiting the Foreign Office to canvass support for the faltering Middle East peace initiative.

It did not seem the best of omens for our own peace process. How distant it all seems now: the historic handshake on the White House lawn just three months ago. How uncertain and difficult the way has proved for Arafat himself and his people.

Can the Downing Street Declaration, as it is already being described, bring an end to violence by Christmas? Or within a year? Or ever? Sitting in the pretty panelled salon overlooking St James's Park, listening to the note of urgency in the voices of both prime ministers as they appealed for generosity and courage "to find a better way ahead, particularly for the next generation", it seemed unthinkable not to respond to their hopes for a new beginning in Northern Ireland.

Their joint statement has been crafted with enormous skill

and commitment by officials on both sides determined to meet the needs of both communities. There is much emphasis on consent, co-operation, dialogue and agreement. In one section, the words "agreed" and "agreement" appear no fewer than 10 times, usually in relation to the need for Unionist consent. However, the thrust of the document is towards a nationalist agenda, a process as outlined so often by John Hume, which will involve people of the island of Ireland alone in working out their future together.

In the House of Commons and in off-the-record briefings to journalists and MPs, the British government's line was that there had been no major concessions to Sinn Féin and that some of its demands had been rejected.

But watching the Unionists in parliament, listening to James Molyneaux, his voice seeming to shake as he read from a prepared script, it was clear that they saw this as yet another step in the long route towards betrayal which started over 20 years ago with the end of Stormont, through Direct Rule, Sunningdale and the Anglo-Irish Agreement.

Section four of the declaration in particular embraces many of the ideas contained in the two statements issued by Hume and Adams during their recent talks. It does so in language which both men will recognise; "Humespeak" is how those who don't entirely admire the SDLP leader describe it.

This section repeats the principle that the British government has no selfish, strategic or economic interest in Northern Ireland, accepts the right of the Irish people to self-determination, emphasises the urgent need to achieve peace, stability and reconciliation and says that the role of the British will be to facilitate and enable the achievement of such an agreement through a process of dialogue and co-operation based on full respect for the rights and identities of both traditions in Ireland.

At the press conference, and later at the Irish Embassy, the question everybody was asking was: "Will it be enough for Sinn Féin to deliver the IRA?" This was given added urgency by the fact that politicians and officials from both sides, still shell-shocked from the negotiating process of recent weeks, were at pains to emphasise their belief that this document represents the limit to which the British government is prepared to go in trying to reconcile the conflicting demands of meeting their responsibilities to the Unionists and offering enough to Sinn Féin to bring them into the political process.

Writing within hours of the announcement, and before Sinn Féin has come forward with any considered response, it is difficult to assess what the reaction is likely to be on the streets of Derry and west Belfast. As always, the response of both nationalists and Unionists will be affected by the degree of approval or outrage shown by the other side.

There will be those within Sinn Féin who will argue that they have already come a very long way since the first joint statement issued by Hume and Adams last April. Much of what was contained in that has now been absorbed into the official policy of the British and Irish governments.

Why not wait a bit longer, they will say, and see if the British can be persuaded to move closer to Sinn Féin on such thorny issues as whether self-determination should embrace the island of Ireland as a whole? That seemed to be Gerry Adams's position last weekend when he speculated in several interviews that the British government would not be prepared to go far enough and that the peace process would take rather longer than the hopes expressed by Mr Reynolds.

But the Sinn Féin leader will know that this declaration by the two prime ministers is likely to command widespread popular support in the nationalist community North and South. John Hume has already endorsed it in his speech in the House of Commons. If Sinn Féin rejects it out of hand, the party will face a period of grim political isolation, exacerbated by the knowledge that any escalation in the IRA's campaign is likely to provoke a reaction of loyalist violence directed against Catholics.

Whatever about the solid loyalty of its own core support, there will be many in the broader nationalist community who will feel that the joint declaration puts it up to the IRA to make a historic gesture to both communities in the North. They will say that the time has come for the Provos to abandon the violence and to use the political process to advance their aspirations, at least if their recent fine words about seeking the agreement of the Unionists are to mean anything.

And yet, even as I write, I cannot forget the figure of Yasser Arafat slipping into the Foreign Office by a side door. Today the Palestinian leader arrives in Dublin. He will be seeking the support of our Government to persuade the Israelis to honour their pledges about withdrawing from the Gaza Strip and the town of Jericho which he hopes to make the capital of a new state for his people.

In yesterday's *London Independent*, in a chilling report from Hebron, Robert Fisk described the apparently irresistible rise of Hamas, the Islamic revolutionary movement which sees the deal that Arafat struck with the Israeli Prime Minister, Yitzhak Rabin, as a bitter betrayal. He saw freshly painted graffiti on the wall of Hebron's Islamic university which read: "Our guns are speaking and will strike down the seller of our country." The seller, he explained, is Arafat.

The lesson of the PLO leader will not be lost on Gerry Adams, Martin McGuinness and those close to them. They came to prominence as a result of a bitter split in the Provos and their first priority, even more than peace, will be to ensure that the same thing does not happen again. They are reasonably confident that the British government will talk to them sooner or later, just as it has in the past.

Against that they have to weigh up the cost of turning

down this offer to their own supporters and what such an act will do to their hopes of establishing dialogue with the Unionist community. It may take them some time to decide. We have already been warned of the danger of setting unrealistic deadlines and it seems unlikely that we will get peace by Christmas. But the joint declaration, issued in Downing Street yesterday, is a brave attempt to help us along that road and has brought peace closer.

1994

Families in failed marriages need understanding, not criticism

JANUARY 27, 1994

I've been wondering all week whether "What about the Children?" – Kathryn Holmquist's series on the conse-quences of separation and divorce – would ever have been published in this newspaper if the parents of the children in question had been travellers, or single mothers, or the unemployed.

I suspect not. I think that if the attitudes to separated parents, which ranged from the harshly judgmental to the insufferably smug, had been expressed about any other group, someone in the editorial hierarchy would have realised just how gratuitously offensive they were, and shouted "Stop!".

Ah but, it will be said, these others – single mothers, the unemployed, the physically disabled, or whatever – find themselves in a situation where their misfortune is not of their own making. They are not to blame. Parents who separate or divorce, on the other hand, make a deliberate and socially reprehensible choice, which has disastrous consequences for their children. That, indeed, is the main point which many of the "experts" whom Ms Holmquist quoted at length particularly wanted to make.

Thus: "Love is a matter of discipline and commitment. People who cannot commit themselves to a partner should not be having children" – Caoimhe Nic Dhomhnaill, child psychologist; "Marriage is increasingly seen as a vehicle for personal commitment rather than a commitment to child rearing. People are not taking parenthood seriously" – Dr John McManus, general practitioner; "I would be totally against divorce on demand... People think that marriage gives you a 100 per cent guarantee of happiness and that is nonsense" – Dr Michael Fitzgerald, child psychiatrist.

What these "experts" seem to have in common is that they speak from the personal perspective of a secure and happy marriage. I congratulate them on their good fortune, but would be more impressed by what they have to say if they showed any understanding that those who are not so fortunate are not necessarily morally inferior to themselves.

Some of these marriages are so brilliantly successful that one of the partners has become (*mirabile dictu*!) a "legislator"; it would be interesting to know if the legislating halves of the marriages regard those of their constituents who have separated as "not taking parenthood seriously".

It would also have been reassuring if any of these experts had conceded that even children lucky enough to live in a perfect nuclear family can experience feelings of loneliness and depression, behave rebelliously and be a source of worry to their parents and teachers.

The whole tone of the articles reminded me of the way people used to talk and write about abortion – that the decision to terminate a pregnancy was a deliberate and selfish choice made by an irresponsible woman who set her own pleasure and gratification above all else. That was until doctors and counsellors, with a more intimate knowledge of the coalface, so to speak, insisted on pointing out that for most Irish women, abortion is a lonely and desperate last resort, experienced more often than not with a heart burdened with guilt and grief.

So, as a separated parent, here are a few notes from this particular coalface directed, in all humility, to the "experts", the husbands of the legislators, and perhaps even the legislators themselves. Are you listening out there, Mrs John McManus and Mrs Michael Fitzgerald?

It may be that I have led an irresponsible and selfish life, but I do number among my friends quite a lot of men and women who have become parents and then separated. I can honestly say that I do not remember one case among them where divorce, or separation after a long relationship, has been undertaken frivolously, without accompanying pain and a sense of failure.

That pain and sense of failure have been much more acute when there have been children involved. Parents know very well that children suffer emotions of grief and loss that never entirely go away. Sometimes they stay together because they cannot face inflicting such suffering.

Often because human emotions are messy, and grief and anger are not the best of counsellors, they do not behave as well as they should, either to each other or to the children. But that does not mean that most parents who separate do not want, quite desperately, to do what is best for these most intimately beloved and vulnerable, small human beings. It simply means that they don't know how, or that the process takes time and that they could do with some help.

What they do not need is to be told that they should never have had children if they were not prepared to make a life-long commitment to rearing them. When they had the children, they almost certainly believed that they also had the commitment. Unfortunately, it's intrinsic to the human condition that emotions change, and if the psychiatrists to whom Ms Holmquist spoke do not recognise this, then, I suggest, they are in no position to lecture the rest of us about living in a world of fantasy.

Most parents, who go on trying to do the best they can for their children after divorce or separation, are only too well aware of how far reality has fallen short of the hopes they once had. Dr Fitzgerald is a lucky man that he will never experience the feelings of failure that weigh on a parent who watches a child's grief and distress after separation, knowing that nothing can be done to give back what has been lost.

What the family in this situation needs is practical advice and support, and that means educating people generally to be more understanding and compassionate about marital breakdown, not less. The teacher, for example, who reacts with warmth and sensitivity, making sure that the child of recently separated parents is not teased or bullied in school, can be more important in helping the family through the immediate fallout than any number of professional experts.

Ms Holmquist is to be commended for focusing attention, in the run-up to a referendum on divorce, on the practical steps that can be taken when parents decide to end a failed marriage. But we need to remember, too, that the reason divorce is necessary is that marriages do fail, creating a situation which is often fraught with violence, grief and unbearable emotional tension for the children.

I wondered, as I read these articles, if Dr Anthony Clare would be consulted or quoted. I mention him because I will always remember, with gratitude, something he said to me when I was feeling particularly bleak and inadequate. "Listen," he said, "coping with a teenager can be impossibly tough, even when there are two parents. That's the nature of the relationship. Don't worry so much about the children. Children are extremely resilient. They'll survive."

And they do. They even grow up to be much kinder and more understanding about their parents than the experts, which is something we probably don't deserve but demonstrates, yet again, the generosity of the human heart.

Loyalist violence yet to appear on agenda

APRIL 14, 1994

A high pile of rubble is all that is left of the hall in Meridi Street, a cul-de-sac off the Donegall Road, where Margaret Wright was beaten and shot by loyalists who are said to have believed mistakenly that she was a Catholic. Bunches of flowers lie all along the footpath. On Tuesday, children were playing among the broken bricks and dust. Further down the road, close to Sandy Row, there is graffiti which makes very uncomplimentary references to the Orange band which used the premises for practice.

The killing has horrified the staunchly loyalist local community. Margaret Wright came from Glencairn, a bleak, windswept estate at the top of the Shankill Road where levels of social deprivation are as bad as anything on the Falls. It is very difficult for people to understand how the killers could have believed that she was a Catholic. A number of people were charged yesterday in connection with the crime, though it seems all too likely that the bloody fallout from the incident is not over yet.

But what happened to Margaret Wright, the fact that police believe she was savagely beaten and killed in front of a number of onlookers, has had a considerable effect on the

Catholic community too. Part of the impact is psychological. Rightly or wrongly, there is a widespread perception that the expressions of horror and revulsion which have come from all levels of the Protestant community are inspired, at least in part, by the fact that the victim was herself a Protestant.

Two years ago, a young Catholic woman, Anne Marie Smyth (26), was murdered in very similar circumstances to last week's killing. According to the police, when her body was found dumped on waste ground in east Belfast, her throat had been cut. Last week, her father expressed his obviously heartfelt sympathy for Margaret Wright's family, but spoke too of his sense of bewilderment and hurt that the reaction of the Protestant community to his own daughter's killing had been so much more "muted". No Unionist politician or church leader in east Belfast had "disowned" those who had been responsible for her terrible death, he said. He told the *Irish News*: "There were over 200 people in the club where Anne Marie Smyth was last seen alive that night, but there was not one wrote a letter to say they were sorry." There was, he said, no reaction in the area. The club was not closed, he said, even for one night.

Whatever about the feeling of hurt in the Catholic community, there is also a pressing sense of physical fear. Meridi Street where Margaret Wright was murdered is less than five minutes' drive from the Falls Road. Many Catholics who live in west Belfast believe that the security forces are either unwilling or unable to protect them from loyalist attacks emanating from the area. Last weekend, there were four attacks on the homes of Catholics, in two of which bombs were thrown into houses as children slept.

These attacks are part of a pattern which is now well established. Last year, there were 84 violent deaths in Northern Ireland connected with "the troubles". Of these, 37 murders were committed by the IRA and the INLA, and 47 by loyalist paramilitaries. For the first time, nobody was killed by members of the security forces. Apart from the Shankill Road bomb, which killed nine passers-by, most of the IRA's victims were either members of the security forces or people who worked for them. I am not excusing these deaths nor attempting to minimise the grief suffered by the families left to mourn them. I know very well that members of the Protestant community experience the IRA campaign as sectarian and directed against them. But what emerges from the news reports, again and again, is the random nature of most of the loyalist attacks on Catholics who have no connection with the conflict, many of whom have been murdered while watching television with their children, or on their way to work.

The optimistic scenario, of course, is that all this will stop if the IRA calls off its campaign, that loyalist violence is "reactive". But this is by no means certain and recent reports by Gerry Moriarty in this newspaper on the mood within the loyalist paramilitary organisations do not encourage one to be sanguine. On the contrary, their spokesmen make it clear that they are deeply mistrustful of the Downing Street Declaration and would regard any future ceasefire, including the yearned-for "permanent cessation" of violence, as signalling that a deal had been done between the British government and IRA, selling out the Protestant community. This, they emphasise, is something they are determined to resist.

How would Catholic areas be policed and protected if the IRA were to call off the violence? This is one of a number of hard, practical problems which is rarely raised when the peace process is debated and discussed. There seems to be a tacit understanding between both governments that policing, the release of prisoners, gradual demilitarisation, are matters for discussion further down the road, when the violence ends. Yet these issues are probably more important to most of the people whom Sinn Féin represents than whether the right to self-determination will be exercised by the Irish people collectively or in separate units, North and South. It would make the prospects for peace seem much more credible if they were brought onto the agenda now.

Reminder of inequity in State's extended "family"

MAY 12, 1994

SOME years ago, a friend of mine, a hardworking, law-abiding Dublin woman arrived at my door with a startling request.

Would I, she asked, please find out for her how to get in touch with the IRA? Evidently distressed, she was also quite serious about it.

When we were sitting down, having a cup of tea, she told me why she felt driven to contemplate such a desperate course of action. She was a single mother trying, as best she could, to bring up her son in a Corporation estate in north Dublin. No, not Ballymun, though I'll come back to that subject later.

Her life was already quite hard and she was now at the end of her tether in her relationship with one particular family who seemed bent on aggravating, to put it mildly, their neighbours. There were the usual problems of deafeningly loud music played into the early hours of the morning, sounds of violent quarrelling, and verbal abuse when she or others complained about these things.

A young man who lived alone and seemed socially withdrawn had been singled out as a particular target. Graffiti was daubed on his walls, rubbish piled outside his door was set on fire, and so on. When she remonstrated with the offenders, she was told, in no uncertain terms, to mind her own business or else.

Their attentions had now been transferred to her son, who was jeered at and physically bullied on his way to and from school. Burning paper had been pushed through her letterbox. She did not feel she could leave the child alone, even for a brief period. Already under great stress, it seemed to her the last straw when the family moved a horse into the flat directly above hers and the animal's hooves could be heard through the uncarpeted floor.

"Hold on," I said, sitting in the kitchen of my suburban house. "There must be a solution to this."

"What do you suggest?" she said.

She had already been to the Garda Síochána. They had told her that there was very little they could do in a private dispute between neighbours unless provable physical violence was involved. They advised her to take a private action through the courts. She had the impression that they regarded the whole area as Indian territory.

She then went, as she had done on several previous occasions, to Dublin Corporation to beg for a transfer out of the estate. As a single woman with one child she did not have enough points to qualify for this. She had attempted to explain her problems to at least one local politician. He had referred her to the gardaí. Now, after a sleepless night listening to the horse and with a child in tow who had refused to go to school, she was looking for more direct action.

What did I do? Well, let's say we didn't need to involve the IRA. Fortunately, the name of *The Irish Times* carries some weight and when I rang the office of one of her local TDs, who just happened to be the serving Taoiseach, steps were taken to solve the problem. At least, a flat in a different estate became available.

I thought of writing about it at the time, as a story illustrating what happens to people if the institutions of the State fail to respond to their absolutely reasonable demands for some degree of security in their living environment. I didn't for two reasons.

The first was that I knew from experience that Dublin is a very small place and that, even if I went to some pains to disguise my friend's identity and that of the estate on which she lived, somebody would be sure to recognise her and she didn't want that. The second was a queasy fear of complaints that, writing from the smug, patronising comfort of my middle-class suburban home, I had cast a wholly unwarranted and hurtful slur on an entire working-class community doing its best, admittedly against some difficult odds, to build a life together.

What has happened to Roddy Doyle highlights a dilemma which has faced almost every journalist who tries to report on problems of economic and social deprivation, wherever they occur. It's been particularly evident this week walking around Ballymun, talking to people who live there and to those who have worked to try to make it a better place in which to live and bring up children.

On the other hand, these people are fiercely eager to make you understand that things have improved greatly in recent years, that all kinds of things have happened to create a new sense of hope in Ballymun. They talk of the work that is being done in community development, of the programme for refurbishing the flats, of the fact that some new shops have opened in the Ballymun Town Centre.

Crucially they explain that the housing shortage in the rest of Dublin means that people are prepared to live in the estate and that there is some real sense of a settled community. And, of course, all these things are true, just as it is true that the vast majority of people who live in Ballymun are "indomitable" in their determination to overcome the economic and social odds against them.

Then, almost in the same breath, the very same people tell you that the drug problem is "completely out of control", that intimidation is rife, that unemployment runs from over 40 per cent in the new flats to 89 per cent in some of the older tower blocks. They talk about the problems of young families in an area where more than 70 per cent of the births are to single mothers.

And there is plenty more which they don't have to tell you because the evidence is there for all to see – the sense of physical desolation, the supermarket which due to the "negative response" of its customers charges a £5 deposit on a trolley to carry the shopping, the kids lounging in entrances drinking cider.

It is arguable that a drama series like *Family*, far from being too hard on Ballymun, does not go far enough in documenting the social, economic and political problems with which the people who live there have to struggle. But at least it forces the rest of us, journalists and readers alike, to feel shame that our fellow citizens arc still living in such conditions and perhaps even to demand the political action necessary to change them.

Time has come to draw line under past

If it is over – and I do believe, that with the help of a fair wind, the peace can last – why do I wake up in the morning with a knot of tension in my stomach threatening the song in my heart?

Sitting in RTÉ on Wednesday night, I watched, on the large screen, the revellers on the Falls Road, flags waving, and the noise of car horns filling the night. Did they really feel such splendid confidence in the future that their celebration of the IRA's statement seemed more like a victory rally?

Talking to people on the second day of peace, it seems that the first jubilation has been replaced by a quieter and more apprehensive mood. Peace is a foreign country and a generation of young people have grown up in the North who have no maps to guide them. It is going to take a long time before they, and we, feel quite comfortable with its unfamiliar contours.

I don't mean simply that there is a natural caution about what might happen, or not happen, in the weeks ahead, though that is obviously crucial. If the loyalists stay reasonably calm, if John Major acquires some of the bold generosity which has been demonstrated not only by the Taoiseach but by his political opponents, if the sceptics within the nationalist community do not destabilise the fragile equilibrium with their accusations of a sellout – then we are in with a good chance.

But the deeper emotional problems of coming to terms with peace after 25 years of conflict are only just beginning to emerge. In this newspaper yesterday, Dick Grogan talked to people on both sides who have been left bereaved by the violence. Some of them, like Gordon Wilson, have demonstrated an inspiring generosity which is rooted in their deep Christian faith.

Others, quite understandably, cannot manage that. They feel bitter and their sense of pain and loneliness has been made more intense by the scenes of Gerry Adams being greeted as a peacemaker on the Falls Road. Many thousands of people in both communities have been made to remember grief and confront desperate emotions which they have tried over the years to put behind them.

Adding to this there is uncertainty. War, for all the damage it inflicts, binds a community together in a quite extraordinary way. People are kinder, more tolerant of each other in the face of the threat from a common enemy.

We have been accustomed in this country to jeer at the nostalgia with which the British remember the blitz on London during the last war, but anyone who has been in the North in the aftermath of some terrible atrocity knows very well that the sense of crisis does bring out the best in people.

The loyalist community in particular, although it has suffered so much at the hands of the IRA, has also derived a certain security from the knowledge that Britain would not abandon it while it was vulnerable to terrorist violence. Now that costly reassurance has been removed.

There is a terrible allure to war and we should not under-estimate it. Northern Ireland, for all its grim reputation, has been on the world stage and sometimes at its centre for 25

years. Unremarkable provincial towns have become accustomed to television cameras recording the moves of local
heroes and heroines, who will soon have to accept that peace
will mean a return to obscurity.

George Eliot remarked that the happiest nations have no
history. Will we come to believe it? We pore obsessively over
our history, picking over the bones in endless discussions
about Irish identity. Look at the themes of the summer schools
that stretch from one end of the country to the other. John
Hume, among others, has said that the time has come to draw
a line under the past and to look to the future. Let us hope
that, after 25 years, we are able to rise to the challenge.

1995

Frightened women may get only fudge and a list

MARCH 2, 1995

I have been thinking a lot about Mr S over the past week. Although it is 20 years since I last saw him, standing at the bottom of my bed in a shabby London hospital, I remember him as clearly as though it were yesterday.

A big, bluff man of military bearing, he always looked as though his white coat had shrunk two sizes in the wash. Nurses danced attendance on him, as was the custom in those days, and medical students treated him with deference, for he could be sharp with them. But, to his patients, women drawn mostly from a poor area of north London, many of them emigrants who could not speak English, he was unfailingly kind and courteous.

Mr S was a senior obstetrician in a large and rather run-down teaching hospital. My GP, who sent me to him when I was pregnant with my first child, told me that not only was he a superb doctor, but he was committed to the National Health Service. He looked after me during both my pregnancies. During the first, he was quite disapproving of the fact that I was travelling regularly from London to Northern Ireland, to cover the conflict that was emerging between the British army and the Provisional IRA. I was aghast when he offered to write to the editor of the newspaper for which I was working to say that I should not be sent on such assignments.

It was at a time in the early 1970s – when women like myself still felt we had to prove that a little thing like pregnancy wouldn't get in the way of the job. I told him this and he said gravely: "You know, all that matters now is what is good for your baby."

During the second pregnancy, I had to spend quite a lot of time in hospital. I always suspected that this was because Mr S was afraid that I might go into labour during a riot in Ballymurphy. Like many women, trapped in hospital with nothing to do, I became obsessed with the idea that there was something wrong with the foetus. One of the nurses had told me that the head seemed rather large and I told Mr S of my fears. "Nonsense," he boomed. "You've got a fine bouncing boy in there, I should think." Then, realising that I was not reassured by this, he instructed his registrar to organise a test and, when the results came through, came back up to the ward himself to explain to me that there was nothing to worry about.

Later, when my son was born, he came to see me. "Well! Well! I was right, wasn't I?" he shouted, beaming with pleasure.

But the reason I have been remembering him with such gratitude over the past few days has nothing to do with these sentimental memories of happy motherhood. Rather, I recall how he treated me with this same kindness and consideration when I went to tell him that I was pregnant and wanted a termination. His reaction was complex. We talked for quite a long time and it was not exactly non-directive counselling. He obviously viewed the idea of abortion with extreme distaste.

Thinking about it later, I understood that this was a man of great skill and generosity who had chosen to work for relatively modest rewards in the National Health Service. Money was never mentioned in his relationship with his patients. He was fulfilled in his job because he believed that he was truly privileged, every day, to assist at the miracle of birth. But again, when he understood that for me this was a real crisis and that I couldn't cope with it, he treated me as a patient who needed his help, right through to visiting me after the operation to make sure that I was all right and to say that, if I needed help, I knew where to reach him.

What has puzzled me in recent days, as the abortion debate has surfaced once again, is this: how can it happen that Irish women still have almost no chance of being given the kind of care and respect which I experienced in London more than 20 years ago? Lawyers argue with enviable certainty about the great abstractions. But what do Irish doctors think of the latest proposals put forward by Michael Noonan, which seem to deny that they might feel any sense of responsibility towards their patients, women who come to them frightened and in distress?

The Health Minister has suggested that, when a GP refers a patient to a specialist, he or she often does no more than write a letter of referral, leaving the patient to arrange the appointment. Every family doctor worth his or her salt knows that this is a caricature of what happens. Even in cases of quite minor importance the GP chooses the consultant, tells the patient why this particular specialist is appropriate, and what to expect when the consultation takes place. This is a long way from presenting a distressed patient with a list of names and addresses in Britain and suggesting that she should pick one of them with a pin.

What will those many conscientious family doctors do, who accept that a woman, after counselling, may opt for abortion? I imagine they will fudge, doing their best to help the individual patient in every practical way, while at the same time hoping that they are not being entrapped. But why should they have to carry out their medical duties in this dishonest and potentially incriminating fashion?

We are not an uncaring people when challenged to respond at a human level on issues of this kind. Our reaction to the X case showed that clearly.

When the Supreme Court ruled that the young girl should be allowed to have her pregnancy terminated, the overwhelming feeling in the country was one of relief. But translating a compassionate response into meaningful reform requires moral courage on the part of politicians. It can be done. Máire Geoghegan-Quinn demonstrated this in the way she piloted the change to the laws relating to homosexuality through the Dáil.

Perhaps we will have to wait for a woman minister to introduce the laws that will give effect to the Supreme Court decision and make abortion available to Irish women in their own country. That change will come. It is even possible to predict how it will happen.

There will be another case, even more painful and upsetting than that of Miss X. Let us look at last week's news and speculate that it might involve a middle-aged man who has regularly abused one or more of his children. A daughter, already physically damaged, is found to be pregnant by her father and threatens suicide. There is some complication, which means she is unable to travel to England. An Irish doctor carries out an abortion and is prosecuted. There is a wave of public sympathy and he is treated like a hero.

I do not mean to sound either cynical or unduly maudlin. Contrary to what some regular readers of this column may suspect, I do not at all like writing in this confessional fashion, and I find reminiscing about events that happened so long ago and in another country more than somewhat embarrassing. It would be an enormous relief if some younger woman or women were to start writing about the issue of abortion from personal experience and leave me to the relatively easy task of analysing the peace process. Please.

Did Dev save the soul or skin of Ireland?

MAY 4, 1995

The end of the Second World War in Europe was marked in our family by a monumental row. I wasn't present at the incident which sparked it off, and only pieced together what happened in accounts given to me, in some cases many years later. I don't even know exactly when it happened, though it must have been some time after de Valera's visit to the German consulate to present his condolences on Hitler's death.

The episode involved my mother, home from England where my father was serving in the British army, and an uncle, who was parish priest in the part of west Cork which was home originally to both sides of the family. I know that he was well respected – if somewhat feared – and regarded with deep affection by his congregation.

On this particular Sunday, my uncle preached a sermon at Mass, giving thanks for the end of hostilities in Europe and praising de Valera for his courage and wisdom in following a policy of neutrality. By keeping this State out of a European war, he said, "de Valera saved Ireland's soul".

It seems that my mother grew increasingly agitated during the course of his homily. The reason soon became clear. At the end of Mass, when my uncle was standing at the church door greeting members of his flock, she marched up to him and said: "De Valera may have saved your skins, but it was English cockneys who saved your souls."

There was consternation. Letters were written to my father in England complaining, first, about my mother insulting the priest at his own church door and, second, about her extraordinary views. He was absolutely furious with her. It was one thing for him to join up, quite another for her to provoke a public row with his brother, the priest, on the issue.

Many years later, when I was covering the conflict in Northern Ireland and such questions became once again a matter of life and death, I often thought of how my mother and my uncle, both of them products of the same environment and bound to each other by family ties, could have held such passionate and conflicting views on a war in which Ireland was not directly involved.

Both of them had lived through historic times, known many of the people involved in the struggle for independence in their own county of Cork. But my mother's attitudes had been complicated by the experience of living through the final years of the war with ordinary Londoners. She was affected and changed by finding that, although they were often venal and shockingly relaxed in their sexual attitudes, they were also capable of a generosity, tolerance and moral stoicism which owed nothing to the teachings of any church.

She would have been moved by last Friday's simple ceremony in the Memorial Park at Islandbridge and by the whole tenor of John Bruton's speech. Not so much because it was an occasion when this State finally reclaimed the Irish men and women who fought and died in both world wars, nor even by the presence of a Sinn Féin representative alongside members of the Jewish community, but because the Taoiseach finally confronted the characteristics, which he described as common to all of us, that closed the doors and the ports to Jewish refugees.

It was enough for the day that was in it. But an outside observer might have added that even the closing of the doors was not neutral, that some refugees were a lot more equal than others. In these days, when it seems that the situation in the former Yugoslavia is spiralling out of control, we in Ireland must not forget Andrija Artukovitch, whose terrible story was revealed only through the moral courage and tenacity of the late Hubert Butler.

Artukovitch was Minister of the Interior in the independent state of Croatia, a puppet regime which operated under Hitler's protection from 1941. His main task was to run the Ustase, the Croatian equivalent of the Gestapo, whose enthusiasm for "purifying the territory" of Jews, Romanies and, principally, Orthodox Serbs surprised even their Nazi masters.

Concentration camps were set up in which 30,000 Jews and their rabbis perished. But this figure paled into insignificance beside the numbers of Orthodox Serbs who were offered the choice of converting to Catholicism or death.

After the war, the Yugoslavs wanted to put Artukovitch on trial as a war criminal. With the help of the Franciscans he made his way, disguised as a priest, first to Rome, and then to Switzerland. But not even the Swiss, who were inclined to leniency on such matters, were prepared to give him sanctuary. He was given two weeks to leave the country.

Again, the church came to his aid and an approach was made to the Irish consulate in Berne, which arranged for him to come to Dublin. He and his family spent a year in Rathgar, where his youngest son was born in 1947.

Everyone who met Artukovitch told Hubert Butler that he

was "a wonderful husband and father" who "lived only for his family". In 1948, travelling on an Irish identity card issued by the Department of External Affairs, he went to California where he was absorbed, honoured even for the way he had opposed communism.

The Yugoslav government made repeated attempts to have him extradited. On one occasion, he was saved by a petition signed by 50,000 members of the Knights of St Columbus. Finally, after a series of civil suits had been brought against him by relatives of Jewish refugees "killed in the death camps", Andrij Anitch (aka Artukovitch) was sent back to Yugoslavia in 1986. He was tried and sentenced to death, but his age and physical infirmity saved him and he died in prison in January 1988.

This is not a story of 50 years ago. Artukovich died seven years ago. Three years later, in June 1991, Croatia seceded from Yugoslavia. Shortly afterwards, Ireland went along with the decision of the European Community, taken after intense canvassing by Germany, to recognise Croatia's independence, despite the deep misgivings expressed by the United States.

As always, we had the excuse that we are a small, unimportant state and that these are issues for the big powers. But do we think, even now, as each evening on television the Serbs defend their latest actions by saying that Croatia is a client state of Germany and one which has the backing of the European Union, that this is an issue with which we have an intimate connection?

None of this is intended to justify the atrocities that have been committed in the name of Serbian nationalism in the former Yugoslavia, least of all this week's merciless bombing of Zagreb.

It is an attempt to argue that there is no such thing as neutrality. Every decision taken by this State in the field of foreign affairs has moral and political implications which we cannot shrug aside, much as we might like to do so. That was true in 1940 and remains so today. Perhaps the most hopeful development of last week was that both Bertie Ahern and John Bruton, in their different ways, tried to spell this out for us.

Putting past behind to give peace a chance

JUNE 1, 1995

*"I get down on my knees and do what must be done
And kiss Achilles' hand, the killer of my son."*

These are the closing lines of 'Ceasefire', one of the poems from his marvellous new collection, *The Ghost Orchid*, in which Michael Longley writes with almost unbearable tenderness of the pity of war and of the terrible pain of making peace.

In a series of poems drawn from *The Iliad*, he reworks the intimate, familial episodes: the parting of Hector and Andromache, the terror of their baby son when he sees his father dressed and armed for war, Hector's prayer that the boy will grow up to be strong and brave, "bloodier" in battle than himself.

The poem, 'Ceasefire', will surely be read and remembered, taught to schoolchildren and quoted long after our present Troubles have become a distant memory. The poet's theme is taken from the last book of *The Iliad* when King Priam, desolated by the death of his son, goes to Achilles' tent to beg for the return of Hector's body.

His own people, knowing Achilles to be maddened with

rage and grief by the death of Patroclus, beg him not to go. But Achilles, moved by Priam's appeal and by memories of his own father, mingles his tears with those of the old king and himself dresses Hector's body for the return to Troy.

But first there is the necessary act of grace without which no healing peace is possible, when Priam puts to his lips the hands of the man who has killed his son.

I remember talking, during a particularly bleak period of the violence in the North, to a Presbyterian minister in County Tyrone whose congregation felt itself to be living under a permanent sense of threat. It could as easily, of course, have been a Catholic priest from a neighbouring parish. He had noticed, the young man said, that the people who had suffered most directly from the violence, through the loss of a loved relation, were almost never bitter.

It was as though they received some special grace which enabled them to see that the grief which they felt would be defiled if they were to wish for others to suffer in the same way. It was those on the periphery, not directly affected, who spoke of the need to inflict revenge on "the other side", to teach them a lesson, thus ensuring the continuing spiral of mistrust.

We are moving into a particularly challenging stage of the peace process just now. The early reactions of euphoria and relief that the guns are silent and that the ever-present fear of violence has lifted, have to some extent faded away. People are growing impatient, demanding more tangible evidence that things have changed and that there is no going back.

But if we are to achieve the transformation from the absence of war to a true inclusive peace, it will take more than political ingenuity and courage, rare and desirable though those qualities may be. It will require the capacity for forgiveness which continues to elude most of us, and the imagination to understand and seize the opportunities for making the peace.

We all recognise the act of grace which moves the situation irreversibly forward. Sometimes we see it in individuals – Gordon Wilson's response to the death of his daughter, the generosity of Tim Parry's parents, the extraordinarily forgiving attitude of the people of Loughinisland after their village was most cruelly attacked.

At other times it can be glimpsed in governments and politicians – Sir Patrick Mayhew's handshake with Gerry Adams, Sinn Féin's decision to send a representative to the ceremony at Islandbridge commemorating the Irish who died in two world wars, difficult enough for the individuals involved, but evidence of a determination to reach out and take the hand of a former enemy.

These are the acts of generosity which give substance to the hope that it will be possible to create new and happier relationships on this island. But we can recognise too the opportunities that are missed, by all of us, when we continue to nurse old grudges and to dwell on the wrongs that have been done to us, often in a long distant past which we must, sooner of later, steel ourselves to forgive, if not forget.

It was Maurice Hayes, who has himself done so much to build bridges between the two communities in the North, who gave me a first sight of Michael Longley's new poems, touching on these and other painful matters, at last week's conference on Trade and Investment in Washington.

There is no doubt that the political interest of the United States administration, and its overwhelming goodwill, will continue to influence the direction and the pace of events in the peace process. To take the most obvious and pressing example, the emphasis which President Clinton put on the decommissioning issue, and on the related problem of punishment beatings, must force both of these up the political agenda, and this will present difficulties for Sinn Féin.

Recognising the risks which the US President has already

taken for the party, Gerry Adams and his colleagues may be forced to reassess their policies on these issues and to take what has seemed an impossibly difficult step forward to prove their commitment to peace, and to the even harder task of reconciliation.

But the real importance of last week's conference seemed to me to lie elsewhere. I have been to very many similar gatherings, albeit not quite so large or so glitzy, over the past twenty years and am now well past the stage of being impressed by politicians of passionately conflicting views and backgrounds joining together in singing 'The Fields of Athenry'.

That is not to say I don't enjoy it. I usually do, particularly if the hour is late and the wine is flowing. But I have also lived long enough to know that, in the past, such harmony usually proved to be a fleeting fancy, and that the sweetest singers all too often returned to hurling abuse at each other across the sectarian divide once they returned to this small island.

Perhaps I am being absurdly optimistic, or am too much influenced by the overwhelming goodwill of the American hosts, but it did seem to me that the atmosphere was different this time and that this was due, naturally enough, to the ending of the violence. It wasn't the late-night partying, or the warmth of the various receptions on offer.

More impressive, precisely because they were low-key and did not demand to be noticed, were the meetings and encounters one saw, and sometimes joined, in the corridors and the coffee shop, where former political opponents earnestly discussed community projects and cross-Border schemes to improve the practical environment of the people they represented.

Here, it seemed, were people genuinely facing up to the challenge of putting the past behind them in order to transform a temporary ceasefire into a lasting peace.

AIDS scare may make us wary of warnings from altars

SEPTEMBER 14, 1995

"We never thought this could happen in Dungarvan!" The cry of understandable stupefaction on the RTÉ News when the story broke seems certain to figure in every Christmas round up of "Sayings of the Year". It isn't every day that *Fatal Attraction* collides with *Divine Rapture* on the streets of County Waterford, or anywhere else for that matter.

It is easy enough to mock a plot which seems to combine all the elements of a blockbuster crafted by author Andrew Greeley. A handsome young curate, with the slightly pudgy good looks and athletic build of the young Ted Kennedy, a distant cousin whom he might have been well advised to consult on the facts of this particular story before he spoke from the pulpit.

A pretty woman, stricken by plague, prowling the streets hell bent on revenge. She is "petite, dark skinned, with a hint of red colouring in her auburn hair". Deeply sun-tanned, she wears (or used to wear) sleeveless vests which show off the tattoo on her shoulder. Her victims are young men filled with promise and on the threshold of adult life.

The first group, all in their late teens, were meant to go to college this autumn. How many others nurse a secret dread?

161

Fifteen? Fifty? Eighty maybe. But the woman has gone back whence she came – to pagan England – where she lies close to death, her beauty disfigured by the scabs and lesions that mark the last stages of her ghastly disease.

I kid you not. All this stuff has been in the papers. Small wonder that the race is on to cast the movie. Already in the sleek night spots where our most talented film makers gather, the talk is of the availability of certain, obvious stars. Julia Roberts, the original Pretty Woman, has been mentioned for the female lead. A shade obvious, perhaps.

What about Sandra Bullock, the bubbly dark beauty who has had such a hit in *While You Were Sleeping?* For the priest, Tom Cruise has been mentioned – and dismissed as too slightly built, too darkly intense. Brad Pitt's looks are just a shade decadent for Dungarvan. Matt Dillon, who has the blond Kennedy charm and the build of an Offaly footballer, seems a safer bet.

We laugh that we may not weep. At this stage, the story is as full of holes as an official briefing on the breakdown of the Anglo-Irish summit. But the issues it raises – the Catholic Church's attitude to women, the use of the pulpit for rabid scaremongering about sexual issues, the media's sensational and almost wholly credulous coverage of the story do raise questions which are likely to become more, not less, relevant as we move into the campaign on the divorce referendum.

How could it happen that the national media – with a few honourable exceptions – not only fell for the priest's account of what had happened, but treated it with such wild irresponsibility? The main RTÉ News on Monday night sent a camera crew to Dungarvan to talk to local people, but did not have a medical expert to explain that the transmission of the HIV virus occurs rarely in heterosexual intercourse, and that the chances of a man becoming infected by a woman are even less likely.

This is only one example of a failure to check out the basic credibility of the story. RTÉ was by no means the only culprit but, as the national broadcasting station, it might be thought to have a special responsibility not to spread the panic in Dungarvan to a wider audience.

The story should have set alarm bells ringing on other grounds. The stigmatising of "the woman as carrier of infection and disease" is rooted deep in the Judaeo-Christian tradition, but even the Irish Church has tried, to its credit, to move away from the deeply misogynist attitudes of the past.

Yet on this occasion we not only had an anonymous woman (well, sort of anonymous though half the town seems to have claimed that they know her identity) denounced from the altar steps, but journalists almost slavering in their eagerness to pass on the story and the message it contained.

I was present at a number of conferences and conversations immediately after the tale first appeared in the *Cork Examiner*, and before the doubts and qualifications began to surface. What was interesting was that women were immediately horrified by Fr Kennedy's actions and sceptical of his account of what had happened.

Men, even kindly, tolerant, politically correct husbands and fathers, were much more inclined to believe it and to think that the young curate was absolutely right to have behaved as he did. Phrases were used like "it was attempted murder".

It isn't my intention here to use a sledgehammer to attack Fr Kennedy. He seems a kind, if culpably naive man, and one who is genuinely caring about the welfare of his congregation. His confidence will be badly bruised by this experience and this may help him to become a better priest.

The serious questions as to why he failed to inform either the local health board or the Garda will be dealt with by the relevant authorities. Already his bishop is said to be extremely annoyed that he decided to make his shock announcement without informing either the parish priest or his diocesan superiors.

AIDS scare may make us wary of warnings from altars

But Fr Kennedy might feel entitled to argue that he was only following a path already well trodden by the bishops themselves. Last month, the Archbishop of Cashel, Dr Dermot Clifford, took it upon himself to preach on the consequences that could follow the introduction of civil divorce in Ireland.

He warned that divorced men are five times more likely to commit suicide than their married counterparts, three times more likely to have car accidents and are at dramatically greater risk of being committed to a psychiatric institution. Divorced women are three times more likely to attempt suicide than those who remain married.

And that is only the start of it. Children whose divorced parents remarry are seven times more likely to be subjected to sexual abuse in the new family, and to suffer in many other ways. "These are the result of scientific research, some of it very recent," the Archbishop intoned. "They represent statistical evidence."

On the day that Dr Clifford was preaching at the Holy Cross Abbey in Tipperary, Bishop Brendan Comiskey was warning of the consequences that could occur if the voices of the Catholic right were excluded from the national debate on divorce. The Bishop of Ferns cited the Michigan Militia, which has been linked to the Oklahoma bombing, as an example of what could happen if people felt that they had been unfairly silenced.

Compared with this kind of thing, Fr Kennedy's fantastic scaremongering is in the ha'penny place. And there will be a lot more of the same as the referendum debate gathers momentum. Already we have been told that the pulpit will be used as the main forum for informing and educating the faithful on the dangers of divorce.

If the panic in Dungarvan has taught us to be just a bit more sceptical about dire warnings from the altar, Fr Kennedy may have rendered us all a service.

Tongues of fire as hope and history rhyme

OCTOBER 12, 1995

A few days before he learnt that he had won the Nobel Prize for Literature, Seamus Heaney stood in the Greek amphitheatre at Epidaurus. There, like many a visitor before him, he tested the miraculous acoustics of the arena, with its tiers of white limestone seats stretching to the sky.

He chose a play by Sophocles or rather, as he himself put it on his return to Dublin, he spoke some lines which he had, "rather impertinently", added to the original text.

You probably know the lines, gentle reader, for they have been reprinted many times since they were first spoken at the Guildhall in Derry in 1990. Heaney had written them for T*he Cure at Troy*, the version of Sophocles' *Philoctetes* which he had translated for the Field Day Company:

> "History says, Don't hope
> on this side of the grave.
> But then, once in a lifetime
> the longed for tidal wave
> of justice can rise up
> and hope and history rhyme."

Then, at a time when it was hard to discern any hope in the North, when the Birmingham Six and other innocent victims still languished in jail, the lines seemed to ring with pitiable defiance from the stage. The fact that Seamus Heaney, who had described so eloquently the conflict he experienced as a poet torn between "Song and Suffering", felt impelled to write them served only to underline the desolation of those days.

So it has been extraordinarily moving to hear of the poet at Epidaurus, where Sophocles' drama of Philoctetes' terrible ordeal was staged 400 years before Christ, and to know that Heaney's lines have been transformed and vindicated by the coming of peace.

This past week, courtesy of the Dublin Theatre Festival, has been resonant with echoes of that experience. Listening to Fiona Shaw speak the lines of *The Waste Land* in the Phoenix Park, watching her splendid physical grace, I remembered seeing her play Electra in a sports stadium in Derry, her body hunched and distorted with grief.

I am not for a moment suggesting that Ms Shaw's performance then was inspired or influenced by the violence in the North, for the production was first staged by Deborah Warner for the Royal Shakespeare Company. But I do know that the few days she spent in that place at that time constituted an experience which she and those who acted with her will never forget.

In the previous week, six people had been killed in Derry. Night after night, the terrible stillness of the audience during the performance erupted into passionate debate on the subject matter of the play – violent death, filial loyalty and retribution.

One evening, a woman took Fiona Shaw's hands and said: "You must not harbour these terrible feelings of bitterness and revenge. We have all of us to try and forgive, to put the past behind us. Otherwise there is no hope" – for all the world as though she was talking of an act of savagery which had happened just down the road, rather than to an actress about her performance in a Greek classical play.

But, more than either of these, it has been the revival of Stewart Parker's *Pentecost* which has brought home, most poignantly, the weight that has been lifted from all of those poets, writers, dramatists who have felt impelled to bear public witness to the pain and waste of the past 25 years, and the history that preceded them. Poignant because Stewart Parker died in 1988 and he did not live to see the hope of *Pentecost* realised.

Again, this was a play which seemed impossible to apprehend fully when it was first produced in 1987. Although it was set in the context of a remembered political experience – the Ulster Workers' Strike of 1974 – it spoke of radiant possibilities for a better future. It was difficult, frankly, to share the author's optimism.

The savage flashes of tribal feeling shown on stage by characters who believed they had escaped from "all that" were much more credible than the healing of the final scene.

The writer's own faith, rooted deeply in the Protestant evangelical tradition, believing in the possibility of individual salvation through Christ's grace, seemed too far removed from the grim daily realities of a place where the victims of murder were routinely identified by the labels of religion.

How we are confounded by the artist's prophetic voice! Now, Stewart Parker seems to be speaking not only to the North, but to the island as a whole. When one of the characters says: "Forget the church. Forget the priests and pastors. There is some kind of Christ in every one of us. Each of us either honours or denies and violates Him. What we do to Him is done to ourselves", she might be addressing thousands of Irish Catholics hurt and bewildered by the scandals and sensations of recent months.

Because *Pentecost* opened at the Project Theatre only last night, I went along to a performance earlier this week. A couple of times, before it started and during the interval, people said to me anxiously: "This is only a preview, you know." Their concern was well meant but quite unnecessary.

In Lynne Parker's production for Rough Magic, the performances of the actors are touched by pain and sharp humour and lit by the grace in which the writer, Ms Parker's uncle, dared us to believe. Even to speak of a "performance" seems irrelevant, so great is the power of what happens on the stage. This is more than an act of homage to the writer's memory, it is a celebration of promise fulfilled.

The last scene of *Pentecost* evokes comparison with *Uncle Vanya*, with this difference – Sonya, in her final speech, looks forward to a life that will be "peaceful, gentle and sweet as a caress" when God, in his divine mercy, gives rest. Stewart Parker, speaking through Marian, has a different vision for Belfast: "We have committed sacrilege enough on life, in this place, in these times. We don't just owe it to ourselves, we owe it to our dead too ... our innocent dead. They're not our masters, they're only our creditors for the life they never knew. We owe them at least that – the fullest life for which they could ever have hoped."

To experience Stewart Parker's play in this production is to understand how we have all, artists and audience alike, been stunted by the ghastly circumstances in the North. Like Seamus Heaney at Epidaurus, Parker's lines are a benediction on those who brought an end to the violence and so made it possible to start a process of spiritual – as well as physical and political – liberation from that demeaning past.

This is a play which speaks urgently and directly of the challenge which faces all of us to affirm that liberation. I would hope that Rough Magic could tour it to villages and towns in both parts of Ireland. But failing that, beg, borrow or bribe your way to the Project.

Time has arrived to abolish the Irish solution

NOVEMBER 16, 1995

Fetherlite, Mates, Rameses; in my local chemist's shop, a dizzying array of condoms is displayed on the counter beside the cash register. Nobody going in to buy a tube of toothpaste or a bottle of aspirin can possibly miss them.

How long is it since we were told that if these foreign "engines of fornication" were to become available in Ireland, it would open the floodgates to the contraceptive culture, lead to a devastating increase in teenage promiscuity, and frighten old ladies and horses in the streets? Ten years ago, was it? Maybe fifteen.

O Tempora! O Mores! Now it is seen as a badge of respectability if a young unmarried male carries a packet of condoms. It shows that he has been brought up to be socially responsible, caring enough to take pains not to get his girlfriend pregnant or to run the risk of contracting the HIV virus. The speed with which this change in social attitudes has happened is relevant to the debate on divorce.

It was Charles Haughey who first coined the phrase "an Irish solution to an Irish problem". Interviewed on RTÉ, he said he could not envisage a situation in which single people would be allowed access to condoms. Did he believe this himself? It seems unlikely but that hardly matters now.

In devising the notion of an Irish solution for dealing with difficult moral issues, he made an argument for hypocrisy and fudge which, as voters, a majority of us have embraced gratefully ever since, particularly in the successive referendums in which we have been asked to make a choice.

Unwanted pregnancy? Sure, have an abortion, just don't have it in Ireland because we have a unique respect for human life here. Pagan England will deal with it for you; get rid of the foetus and nobody need ever know.

Broken marriage? Get a divorce abroad or a church annulment or, if all else fails, have a second family. It's all socially acceptable now. Just don't expect the State to take any hand or part in recognising this new situation because we believe in the beautiful ideal that Christian marriage is for life, whatever the evidence to the contrary.

So, we now have a situation where members of the Oireachtas, of all parties, have obtained divorces and remarried abroad, giving two fingers to the spirit of the Constitution, if not the letter of the law. The leader of the largest political party is separated from his wife and lives openly in a second relationship.

Nobody says, or at least not publicly, that this puts a question mark over his fitness to be Taoiseach, should Fianna Fáil form a government after the next election. On the contrary, people praise his courage and one hears a rush of sentiment in the voice of the TV commentator when he is filmed with his children on official occasions.

I don't mean (how could I?) to sound disapproving. People make their own arrangements to deal with personal situations of this kind so as to be fair to all those involved. But I wonder about the message it sends to other citizens, and particularly to young people, when legislators demonstrate so openly that the law is an ass and that they are entitled to find ways of circumventing it which make it look even more irrelevant. Is this an example to the rest of us to pay our taxes, or to avoid ripping off the social welfare, or to obey the laws on drink and driving?

This, it seems to me, is the question on which John Bruton has touched when he talks of the State's moral duty to deal with the problem of marital breakdown as it exists, rather than with some ideal of marriage to which most people in Ireland aspire, but which an increasing number of our citizens, through no fault of their own, have been unable to sustain.

Last Monday night, when I tried to put this argument perhaps inadequately, on RTÉ's *Questions and Answers*, William Binchy said: "You seem to have an absolute fetish about the law." I thought it was an extraordinary comment from a man who holds a Chair of Law in one of our most eminent universities, and couldn't get it out of my mind. After we had finished recording the programme, I asked him whether he did not think it important that a country's laws should command the willing respect – and thus, hopefully, the acquiescence – of its citizens. "It's a very English view," he said, not unkindly.

"Well, that's the ultimate putdown, Mum, in case you hadn't realised," my daughter commented when I told her later. I did know what she meant, actually. I've read the literature, heard the arguments. I know that the Irish attitude to the law is supposed to be more ambiguous, shifting, supple if you like, and full of guile because of our experience as a colonised people.

Sure, don't we imbibe with our mother's milk the suspicion that the law is oppressive and can only be managed by dint of individual ingenuity?

All I can say is that it is not what I learnt from my parents, whose rigorous adherence to the teachings and practice of the Irish Catholic Church informed, for better or worse, our lives. My father believed in rendering, to the exact penny and on time, what was due to Caesar.

There were occasions when we would have wished him to be a little less certain about his principles, more tolerant of our failures to live up to – or even agree with – them. He did not believe, nor did he teach us, that the laws, of either church or State, could be treated as an à la carte menu (to use what is, I believe, the fashionable phrase about Irish Catholicism).

This referendum seems to me to present a defining moment of choice for us as a people. Whatever happens next Friday, the social changes necessary to deal with the increase in broken marriages will come about in Ireland.

One only has to go to one's local chemist's shop to see how the forces of change work. The condoms on display should offer reassurance, because their availability has not led to the collapse of Irish society as we know and love it.

But equally it is important how we choose to go into the future. We can act from fear, as we so often have in the past, and opt for the Irish solution which means, in effect, pretending this country does not have the same social problems which affect all our neighbours. In other words, we can reject divorce. Or we can look honestly at ourselves, at the needs of our people as a whole, and how we must, from time to time, change our Constitution and our laws to meet those needs.

There are other issues at stake next Friday, many of which have been written about in this paper. There is the message which the vote will send about our treatment of religious minorities in this State, our commitment to pluralism, how it will be seen by Northern Unionists and nationalists. But more important than any of these is what it will tell us about ourselves as a people, whether we want to create a more honest, open society – a society capable of facing up to problems as responsible adults try to do every day.

Politicians must forge working relations for peace

NOVEMBER 22, 1995

The South African Deputy President, F W de Klerk, told a revealing story about his first meeting with Nelson Mandela when he spoke at Trinity College on Monday night.

Mr de Klerk was replying to a question that had been put to him by Jeffrey Donaldson, the general secretary of the Ulster Unionist Party (one of several Unionist politicians whom, to their credit, Tony O'Reilly's aides had invited to the lecture). He asked the South African leader what advice he could give about building trust across a divide, with opponents of long standing.

First, Mr de Klerk said, you have to talk, to learn that your opponents are human beings like yourselves. It is important, he stressed, to try to talk at first about relatively uncontentious subjects, leaving difficult problems to one side, to be dealt with when some degree of trust has been established.

The advice was timely on a day when David Trimble, in an interview in the London *Independent,* described Gerry Adams and Martin McGuinness as "the Karadzic and Mladic of Northern Ireland" and said that he could not envisage a situation of having "personal contact with those gentlemen".

Mr de Klerk described how he had arranged to meet Nelson Mandela soon after he himself became head of the National Party, when the ANC leader was still in prison. Mr Mandela was brought to the presidential residence and, after the first introductions, the two men started to talk about South African history.

In particular, they talked about the Anglo-Boer War and, Mr de Klerk said: "I realised that this man had an intricate knowledge of our struggle."

He had already indicated earlier in his speech what that war meant to the Afrikaner community's image of itself. He spoke of its having had to give up the right to national self-determination which had been "won in a bitter struggle in which 25,000 of our women and children perished in concentration camps".

It is an anecdote which tells us as much about Nelson Mandela as about F W de Klerk, if not more. In his autobiography *Long Walk to Freedom*, he remarks on the almost total ignorance of white South African politicians, even relatively progressive ones, of the history of the ANC and the long struggle against apartheid.

But if this is a story about establishing a basis for trust, it is worth noting that it was done to build a professional partnership between two men who were determined to create a new political order in South Africa.

Questioned about the "personal chemistry" between them, Mr de Klerk answered carefully: "It is not a relationship where I would drop in for a cup of tea. We would not go for walks together. It is a working relationship."

Nelson Mandela recalls their first meeting, and what was important about it, differently. He was impressed by F W de Klerk's ability to listen, "a novel experience". On his return to prison, he wrote to his colleagues and, echoing Mrs

Thatcher's description of Gorbachev, said that the new National Party leader was "a man we can do business with".

We look at the televised handshake across a historic political chasm, the pomp and circumstance which attends the signing of treaties, and we want to believe that this is the reality of peace and reconciliation that some healing balm descends from heaven to bring old enemies together in friendship.

It doesn't happen like that. One remembers the moment of hesitation on the White House lawn as Yitzhak Rabin steeled himself to shake the hand of Yasser Arafat. The symbolism is important, to inspire and persuade the rest of us that the yearned-for change is possible. But the hard reality of creating peace is at once dirtier and much more difficult.

In the two fine speeches which he gave in Dublin, Mr de Klerk was at his most interesting and impressive when he talked about the nuts and bolts of the negotiations that led to the Government of National Unity and, in particular, the "mechanisms" which the parties constructed to help protect the process.

He spoke of the need to keep the main leaders relatively apart from the day-to-day negotiations so that they can keep their minds firmly fixed on the long-term strategy, of having small committees of senior officials to find ways of dealing with specific obstacles, of protecting negotiators from the disappointment or worse of their own constituency. And so on.

But he could not conceal, nor did he attempt to, how difficult it had been at times to carry his own people, how close the whole process had come to break down. He thought now that his party had been "too liberal" on the issue of decommissioning illegal arms, but if they had been tougher the negotiations might have broken down.

Nelson Mandela is equally frank about the problems which he and his party faced, particularly as the violence worsened.

There were times when he thought it had been a terrible error for the ANC to abandon the armed struggle before a constitutional settlement was agreed. Even when the negotiations for a new democratic South Africa started, he believed de Klerk was guilty of, at the very least, duplicity.

When he spoke at the Forum for Peace and Reconciliation, Deputy President de Klerk stressed the importance of timing in launching a process of political change.

He had been presented with a moment when the white community in South Africa had come to understand that radical change was necessary and the black community was still willing to accept compromise.

Some of the difficulties encountered in our own peace process have been to do with unfortunate timing of political events.

The collapse of the coalition government headed by Albert Reynolds, the weakness of John Major's Conservative Party in the run up to a general election in Britain have presented real problems to maintaining the momentum.

But it is the job of serious politicians to adapt to, and find ways of dealing with, problems of this kind. If the circumstances really cannot be changed, and that may be so in the case of John Major's present vulnerability, then a new strategy must be devised for dealing with them.

Mr de Klerk was suitably diplomatic when he emphasised that no two situations are quite comparable, that the politics of South Africa are not those of Northern Ireland.

But the more one looks outside, to other countries which have faced terrible problems in the pursuit of peace, the more one is struck by a common factor in their politicians.

Over and over again, whatever their private frustrations, men like de Klerk, Mandela and Rabin say, "There is no turning back now". Often, as if to explain and justify this assertion, they refer to the overwhelming yearning of ordinary people to live in peace.

Gerry Adams has said that, whatever the difficulties it faces, Sinn Féin is committed to taking the peace process forward. But we need to hear it said more often, and by all the parties involved.

1996

Bus bomb may give republican doves room to move

FEBRUARY 2, 1996

"Bombs bring a dreadful sort of clarity." These are the opening words of an editorial on Northern Ireland in the *Economist*, a periodical which not even the chairman of the Fine Gael Parliamentary Party could accuse of "following a Sinn Féin agenda".

Even if I had shared this view, I do not think I would have said so, for fear of adding to the hurt already caused by the bombs. In fact, over this past week, my mind has been filled by memories of funerals in the North and by the fear of having to return to the bleakness of graveyards in winter.

Sometimes an outsider can see the situation much more clearly, precisely because he or she is not vulnerable to emotions of this kind. Who can doubt that the bombs in London have jolted the two governments into a new sense of urgency?

That is still difficult to admit. Here's another unpalatable thought that the second explosion, on a London bus, which seemed at first to confirm a sense of despair, may provide a gleam of hope for the future.

Since that bombing, I have talked to a number of people with a closer understanding of republican psychology than mine. They believe that the explosion on the No. 171 bus could present an important opportunity. There is always within the IRA/Sinn Féin a tension between those who believe that change can be achieved only by violence and those who argue that political methods are more effective.

In recent years, and particularly in the early months of the IRA's ceasefire, Gerry Adams and those who have argued for the political path have been on the winning side. When the ceasefire was perceived as having failed to yield the expected progress, the militarists reasserted their authority. But they, too, have to demonstrate that they can get results.

The first bomb, in London's Docklands, despite the deaths and injuries it caused, was seen within the IRA as a well-planned, efficiently executed operation. The second bomb, defused because adequate warnings had been given, confirmed the impression that the IRA could strike at will in the British capital.

But the third explosion, on a London bus last Sunday night, was seen as a classic "cock-up". Not only did the bomb fail to reach its destination, probably the Old Bailey – but the political fallout has been entirely negative. Images of a Hamas style no warning attack on innocent civilians have been seen across the world. The British police have seized sizeable quantities of explosives and bomb-making equipment.

This, in itself, may be enough to start the pendulum swinging back in favour of Gerry Adams and give the politicians a brief space in which to save the peace. We have to recognise, though, that the room for manoeuvre is now much more limited, and try to respond accordingly. As one politician put it to me last week: "The problem is that more is required from all parties to rebuild trust, just at the time when it is only possible for them to give less."

This applies most obviously to the position of the IRA/Sinn Féin. However devoutly we may yearn for the IRA to pledge itself to a "genuinely permanent" cessation of violence, the terms on offer this time around are likely to be a great deal less satisfactory than those which Albert Reynolds was able to exact 18 months ago. Peace now will be conditional.

Those who believe, as I do, that this is still a prize worth striving for will have to be prepared to defend the politicians who accept it from charges of "appeasement", to point out that an end to violence, however fragile, provides the only basis on which a lasting peace can be built.

There have been hopeful signs even during this dark period. The Sinn Féin leadership has reiterated, again and again, its commitment to seeking a negotiated settlement through peaceful methods. It has signalled that, if assurances were given on a timetable for the start of all party talks, the IRA might be prepared to accept the six principles in the Mitchell report.

Mitchel McLaughlin, on the night after the bus explosion, said on *Questions and Answers* that he believed Sinn Féin would abide by any settlement, provided his party had been involved in the negotiations, and would "sell" such a deal to the IRA. This is a very long way from the pre-ceasefire situation.

But more is going to be asked of Sinn Féin, at least in the immediate future while confidence in the party's bona fides is being rebuilt. If the Taoiseach and the British Prime Minister do manage to find a formula which sets a date for talks, but which involves some form of "elective process", there will be an onus on everybody to try to make it work. Gerry Adams is not the only politician with problems. The weakness of John Major's parliamentary position is deeply unfortunate but it is a reality with which nationalist politicians will have to work.

There are resources on which the Government can call. Of these, by far the most important is the continuing sympathetic interest of the United States. But the American card has to be deployed sparingly and with diplomatic finesse.

Senator George Mitchell arrives in Dublin today. His report still offers the best basis on which all parties could move forward. His authority and the confidence which he has managed to command across the board make him a valued adviser and possible ally for the future. But to suggest he should be asked to play an active role now would be premature and likely to infuriate the British just when it seems John Major may be prepared to move.

It is more important to ensure that the considerable pressure which the United States can bring to bear on the IRA is used to good effect, and preferably behind the scenes. This clout exists at the level of the White House and of the Irish-American lobby which helped to broker the ceasefire; both are important. Discussions which ensure that Gerry Adams is allowed to renew his visa for the United States in return for a commitment from the IRA that it will pull back from violence would have much to commend them.

Some readers will ask: "Why go to such pains to rescue Gerry Adams and Sinn Féin?" In recent days, a number of politicians have started to canvass, once again, the idea of a settlement negotiated between the moderate parties, which excludes the extremists on both sides. The unspoken assumption is that it will be possible later to "smash" the IRA. This is a strategy which has failed for 25 years and which even the British recognised could not succeed.

That is why John Hume, who has tried again and again to make such settlements work, saw that it was essential to bring the Provos in from the cold and started his talks with Gerry Adams. Their joint project to take the gun out of Irish politics once and for all offered us the chance to escape from the past. We have to rebuild it.

Lectures on "welfare fraud" ring very hollow

DECEMBER 5, 1996

In a week when the competition has been heavy, the prize
for political bad timing must go to the Department of Social
Welfare. Yesterday, the *Star* newspaper carried an
advertisement announcing a crackdown on welfare fraudsters.
"People who cheat the system" the Department intoned from a
moral height "are stealing from every taxpayer in Ireland".

Over the past few days, we've been told, Leinster House has
been "awash with rumours" or names of TDs and others who
figure in the Price Waterhouse Report, and who may or may not
have "cheated the system". But the fallout from the Lowry affair
should extend far beyond the question of what names are to be
found in the pages of the Price Waterhouse Report.

The reaction of less privileged citizens will be to wonder
how these people, as individuals or a group, have the nerve to
believe that they are entitled to lecture the rest of us on our
responsibilities. That will apply however far the individual
politician is removed from venality. From now on, it's going to
be hard to take seriously any minister who talks about the need
for wage restraint, the importance of observing the planning
regulations, or of paying one's car tax.

So far, Mary Harney has been the only party leader who has

made this explicit connection, spelt out the damage that this affair has done to the credibility of politicians as a group. She asked how the Dunnes Stores workers, who have been through a number of bruising strikes to extract minimal concessions from their employers, were expected to react to this week's revelations about the sums paid out to politicians.

She might have extended the analogy. If even a few of the rumours turn out to be true, the Lowry affair could have the same impact on the body politic as the spate of scandals that started with the Bishop Casey affair had on the authority of the Catholic Hierarchy.

As with the cumulative effect of the scandals within the Church, this crisis has been a long time in the making. It's not so long ago that people were prepared to accept that the laws on all these issues – payment of income tax, the planning laws, even traffic regulations – were largely "aspirational". They laid out guidelines for the way the State ought to be run, but everybody knew these were regularly breached. It was part of the way we were.

The tolerance extended to politicians, perhaps even started with them. It was seen in people's attitudes to the two men who dominated Irish politics in the 1980s, Charles Haughey and Garret FitzGerald. Each man was capable of commanding enormous affection and respect among his own supporters. But outside these circles there was wide agreement in the popular view of their conduct of politics.

Roughly, Garret FitzGerald was seen as a decent man, too innocent for either his own or the national good, who never made a bob out of politics. Charles Haughey, on the other hand, was as rich as Croesus and had never explained how he made his money. If he'd done that well for himself, one was regularly told, he was probably cute enough to run the country.

Attitudes don't change overnight. As Vincent Browne pointed out yesterday, there has been a series of financial scandals involving low standards in high political places – Greencore, passports for sale, the Beef Tribunal (when only the journalist who had investigated the affairs of the Goodman empire was ever brought to court).

These began the process of eroding the trusting confidence that politicians are, by virtue of their calling or family associations, fit to decide what's best for the rest of us. People started to wonder whether they couldn't do better than vote the way their parents had before them. The election of Mary Robinson as President showed it was possible to defy the party machines and elect a relatively inexperienced candidate to high office.

My own view is that the divorce referendum marked a crucial stage in our political development. The voters were presented with a clear but difficult choice between sincerely held, traditional beliefs that were very precious to many people, and an alternative which would have a dramatic impact on Irish society, not necessarily for the better.

It took a lot of courage to face up to the fact that Ireland had to deal with the problem of marital breakdown in an honest and clear-sighted way and to vote accordingly. It put an end, hopefully, to the notion of an Irish solution to an Irish problem.

There have been other expressions of growing political maturity. People voted for the present Coalition parties in the hope that they would deliver on the promise of more open, less scandal-prone government. Perhaps the most dispiriting experience of the past few days has been to watch how all three party leaders, particularly Dick Spring, who would have been leading the attack on these goings-on in the past, have rushed to draw the wagons round the Government campfire.

That may not be enough to satisfy the voters this time around. All the signs are that they want answers and, even more, want to know that the laws of the land will be enforced rigorously and fairly.

Lectures on "welfare fraud" ring very hollow

While the Dáil has been "awash with rumours" this week, events on the streets of Dublin offer a rather more hopeful perspective. The introduction of tough new traffic regulations on the streets of the capital is, obviously, not a matter of major political importance compared with allegations of scandalously low standards in high places.

And yet, the way these new rules have been enforced is quite striking. Anyone who drives in Dublin regularly, including myself, knows that the traffic regulations are a joke.

I thought there would be real road rage when Operation Freeflow came into effect. Instead, there appears to be widespread acceptance, even welcome for the change, not just among drivers of taxis and buses but from ordinary commuters. It may not last, of course, and it would be wrong to suggest that there are no illegally parked cars. But it does seem that, as long as people see that the rules are being efficiently and generally enforced, they are quite happy to abide by them.

The same thing happened when strict drink-driving regulations were introduced two years ago. On that occasion, there were vociferous protests that they would ruin the publicans, and destroy social intercourse as we know it. In their hearts though, people knew that the new rules made sense and, once it became clear that the Garda was seriously determined to put them to the test, they adapted their drinking habits accordingly.

We know what happened. Serious road accidents were dramatically reduced and public attitudes to driving and alcohol were changed.

If the public can change, so, I suppose, can the politicians. But we have to make sure they know that this time we will tolerate nothing less than true contrition and a firm purpose of amendment.

Christmas wrapping cannot cover the hostility

DECEMBER 19, 1996

Here are some extracts from my Christmas mailbag.

Number 1: "Why don't you go home, you dried-up English c _ _ t? Generations of Irish men and women have fought so we would not have to listen to the likes of you. It's typical of the sleveen mentality of *The Irish Times* that it gives you space to spew out Brit propaganda week after week – and probably pays you too. The sooner you f _ _ k off back to England, and take your chums Trimble and Paisley with you, the better."

Number 2: "Is there no end to your gullibility, wishful thinking and sheer silliness? Pardon my bluntness but I am sick and tired of reading your outrageous thoughts on Northern Ireland in *The Irish Times*. Let me spell out a few home truths: it doesn't seem to occur to you that Sinn Féin/ IRA, the people who have to be treated 'sensitively' – in whose mouths, according to you, butter wouldn't melt – are murderers and bombers whose 'sensitivity' to anyone who crosses them expresses itself in the use of the baseball bat (and that's the lightest punishment they dish out). It's not the Americans, the EU or Uncle Tom Cobley who is keeping the peace in Northern Ireland but the British whom you despise so much."

What? No invitations to share a heart-warming cup of festive cheer? Alas, no. The subject of Northern Ireland does not evoke the generous and sympathetic response which letter writers to this newspaper express so eloquently on other issues.

Some consolation came in a letter from a small country town in East Anglia. "My class are doing a project on issues that affect us today. I have chosen to study the Troubles in Northern Ireland. I am interested in the subject and think it is too easy to blame the IRA for everything." The writer is a 12-year-old. Truly, out of the mouths of babes come words that offer hope and goodwill.

I am exaggerating, perhaps disgracefully. Many of the letters I receive from all parts of this State express a deep sense of anguish about the tragedy in the North and repeatedly ask: "What can we do to help?"

Often those who write are already involved in setting up links that will improve understanding and mutual trust with similar groups in the North. I think humbly of notes received from businessmen in the Border counties, of the work done by the Meath Peace Group, of conferences organised in west Cork and many other places geographically remote from violence.

But there are also the other letters, so hostile and abusive that they must give pause for thought. Because I do believe that at least some of this anger and the intemperance with which it is expressed must be directed, not at me personally, but at the whole appalling, intractable mess of the situation in Northern Ireland and our failure to solve it.

Perhaps I have to believe this as a convenient excuse for not facing up to my own shortcomings as a commentator. It will almost certainly infuriate those who write and telephone

The Irish Times' endlessly patient and tactful Reader's Representative to demand that I be dismissed.

In fact, it was not my intention to write about the North in this last column before Christmas. I'd already drafted an article asking some questions provoked by a story in this week's issue of *Newsweek*, entitled "Ireland – the Emerald Tiger". Specifically, I wanted to try to tease out why, if the economy is booming, there are more homeless people on the streets of Dublin this Christmas than ever before, many of them children involved in prostitution.

There are real risks in the endless stream of self-congratulation that we get from politicians that the Irish economy is set to outstrip just about every other state in Europe – the reports of boom times in the building industry and of record spending on everything from toys to cars at Christmas.

Consciously or not, the effect is to raise ever higher the walls of exclusion that trap those less fortunate than ourselves in the ghetto of poverty. There's already evidence of a hardening in attitudes, for example to the unemployed or to those who find it difficult to make a living on low wages. We saw it in the hysterical reaction to reports of welfare fraud earlier this year, the suggestion by one TD that this constituted a scandal of greater proportions than the Beef Tribunal.

It's a timely subject for this period leading up to Christmas. But, not for the first time, the North seemed to exercise an even more serious claim on this space, precisely because it does provoke such extreme reactions of hostility. As when a difficult relative turns up at Christmas, the heart may sink at the prospect of this truculent presence at the feast but we are honour-bound to try to work out a strategy for dealing with it…

Even at the level of crude self-interest, we can't afford to ignore it. If we don't get peace in the North very soon, there is a serious danger of the situation spiralling back to full-scale violence, of a much more bitter and sectarian nature than we have known in the past.

Pray God it will not happen but if it does we should be under no illusion about the likely effects on the island as a whole. At the very least, we should expect to kiss the economic miracle good-bye and watch the Emerald Tiger bound away to a more congenial part of the international forest.

Multinational corporations are rightly attracted by the high educational standards of the young labour force and the quality of life available to them in both parts of this island. But more than either of these, they need a stable environment in which to operate. We have already seen how the increased spending on security has damaged Northern Ireland's economic prospects this year.

This has happened at a time when peace is still, to all intents and purposes, reasonably secure and nothing very dramatic has happened to scare off international investment. That will change, on both sides of the Border, if the absence of political movement increases the threat of a return to violence.

According to the *Newsweek* article, companies are jostling with each other for space in the International Financial Services Centre in Dublin. Will that happy situation continue if a bomb explodes in a restaurant or bar overlooking the River Liffey?

The North is not a place apart. Its people have shown an extraordinary capacity for generosity and forgiveness. It is they who, somehow, have found within themselves the strength to stop the situation deteriorating into the kind of civil conflict we have seen in Bosnia.

But they are exhausted and dreadfully frightened that the hopes for peace may be slipping away. That disappointment and frustration have led to a deepening of sectarian mistrust over the past year, and this makes the search for a settlement that will allow hope for the rebuilding of trust even more urgent. We cannot give up on it.

Gentle – and less gentle – readers: include the North in your thoughts this Christmas when you pray for peace and goodwill to all men and women.

1997

Irish in Britain are still suffering prejudice

FEBRUARY 27, 1997

"I was questioned and insulted and called a thick Irish Mick. I was struck on the face several times, which broke my teeth, and asked repeatedly to sign a statement saying I was at the farm robbing it… I was disturbed by the night staff every half hour. The meals I received were liberally dosed with salt and I was refused a drink. In the end I had to cup my hands in the lavatory basin and flush the toilet to get a drink of water."

The words of Pat Molloy, who was born in Mayo in 1928 and died in Gartree Prison in 1981, serving a sentence for a crime he did not commit. We know now that it was Molloy's false confession, beaten out of him by the West Midlands Police, which led to three other innocent men serving 18 years for the murder of 13-year-old Carl Bridgewater in 1978.

Paul Foot, who campaigned tirelessly for the men's release, described Molloy as "a gentle man and a skilful carpenter". He had a drink problem and had committed small burglaries, but had always refused to take part in anything that might involve violence. The detectives investigating Carl Bridgewater's murder identified him as the weakest and most vulnerable of those who had been arrested.

They boasted openly that they would "break" him – and they did. Much later, the foreman of the jury said that it was Molloy's confession which "held the case against the other men together. Without it there was nothing."

As this latest tragic miscarriage was, finally, admitted last week, the airwaves were loud with reassurances that such a thing could never, ever happen again in Britain. Safeguards have been put in place. The culture within the police is quite different.

Edward Crew, who is now Chief Constable of the West Midlands force, explained that "words like ethics and ethical behaviour didn't figure much in police practice back in the 1970s. They weren't actually important to us." Now all is changed. Ethical behaviour rules – OK.

But some things don't change, not if you're Irish and living in Britain. It is hard to imagine a more timely coincidence than the publication, within days of the release of the Bridgewater Three, of a report entitled "The Irish Community: Discrimination in the Criminal Justice System".

Drawn up over the past eight months by a number of groups working in Britain – including the National Association of Probation Officers, the Bourne Trust and the Irish Commission for Prisoners Overseas – the report details how Irish people and those of Irish descent fare if they become enmeshed in the toils of the criminal justice system.

They are more likely to be stopped and searched by the police than members of any other ethnic group. They are also more likely to be arrested, to be remanded in custody, and given prison sentences longer than those officially recommended by the courts.

The authors have drawn on independent academic research and surveys carried out by organisations like the Probation Service, as well as on their own experience. These show, for example, that in one North London borough, 14.3 per cent of those stopped by the police in 1994 were Irish, while the figures for the Asian and Afro-Caribbean communities were in the region of 4 per cent to 5 per cent, despite the fact that these two latter groups formed a higher proportion of the total population.

The pattern was repeated in Tony Blair's Islington, where 23 per cent of those stopped and questioned were Irish and where, according to a survey carried out for the Safer Cities Project, "the Irish community is deeply suspicious of the police and do not expect them to be even-handed".

At the end, the writers give 56 case histories which put flesh on the bare and depressing statistics. Here, much abbreviated, are a few of them:

- Michael, aged 52, is from Waterford. He wanted to return home and relatives had organised a job and a ticket for him. He had the ticket in his pocket when he was picked up by the police in Victoria Station, singing. He was held in custody overnight and later admitted to a local hospital with severe bruising. He was not charged with any offence. He has not managed to make it home.

- Anna, aged 25, was leaving a pub with friends. They were stopped by two dozen police in three vans. She was searched in one van and a beer glass which she had taken from the pub was found. She was charged with theft, taken to the police station, strip searched and held overnight. Three police officers gave evidence against her but the magistrate dismissed the case.

- Pearse, aged 20, is from County Kildare. He was found in the grounds of a college eating a pizza. The police accused him of breaking into the building but were unable to produce any evidence. He told them that he was unemployed and sleeping rough. He spent six months on remand for the alleged burglary before being acquitted.

There are dozens of similar cases. Some of them are much more serious. But all of these personal accounts raise questions as to why very many Irish people who come into contact with the law in Britain are subjected to intimidation and worse. Over and over again, what comes across is that the description of a person as "Irish" is deliberately intended to be pejorative.

This report has received very little attention, in spite of the coincidence of its being launched within days of yet another serious miscarriage of justice in Britain involving Irish people. There have been no questions in the Dáil, no concerned editorials urging the Government to make representations to the British on behalf of Irish citizens who believe, with some reason, that they are being discriminated against because they are Irish.

It isn't hard to guess why. These people are emigrants, and emigration simply isn't an issue any more, or not one that politicians want to talk about. The good old emerald tiger economy is booming. We are constantly told that nobody has to leave Ireland these days in order to find work. Look at all the emigrants coming home. We don't even call it emigration any more.

We've invented a new name to put an acceptable gloss on the old reality. The "Irish diaspora" evokes IDA images of highly skilled young graduates, jetting off with their mobile phones to conquer the international money markets before bringing their skills back home.

Except that, as we know, some things don't change. I've written here before, to the point of yawn-inducing boredom probably, about how we seem to have abandoned our emigrants, or at least those who leave for the drearily familiar reasons of unemployment and lack of opportunity. There are tens of thousands of them.

This report on one aspect of the contemporary emigrant

experience is a salutary reminder of just how vulnerable many of them are, out there in the jungle. Surely, the emerald tiger is strong enough to care for all her cubs, those who are forced to go as well as those who stay at home.

Harryville gesture revives hopes for resolution

JUNE 26, 1997

"We are taking Harryville out of the equation of areas that will have to be policed this summer." Canon Sean Scully was explaining why he and his congregation had decided there should be no Mass on Saturday evenings in the Catholic church outside Ballymena until September.

He and they know the decision may be seen as a victory for the loyalist demonstrators who have picketed the church for more than 40 weeks. But they hope, in Fr Scully's words, that "if we can make a gesture of this kind in our community, others in Northern Ireland will do the same".

Some people have questioned the wisdom of the decision. Typically, the Rev Ian Paisley has suggested that numbers attending the church were badly down and people were being bussed in to swell the congregation. But the general reaction, particularly from Unionists, has been one of admiration and gratitude for an act they recognise as generous and brave, precisely because there were bound to be people who would say that Fr Scully and his parishioners had been forced to give way to loyalist pressure.

RUC Chief Constable Ronnie Flanagan welcomed "a sincere

and genuine effort by the congregation to reduce tension". James Currie, the Ulster Unionist mayor of Ballymena, who has visited Harryville to express his solidarity with the Catholic congregation, spoke of "a great move which will give people time and space to think about the issues". They hope Fr Scully's announcement will encourage other groups to be that bit braver, less inclined to cower behind their own tribal parapets.

At a time when the overarching political arguments seem as polarised as ever, it is important to give credit for the good deeds on both sides in a difficult period. Last weekend, three Orange marches passed off peacefully when the marchers accepted RUC restrictions. Robert Overend, the deputy grand master of the Orange Order, appears to have managed a difficult situation at Bellaghy with considerable dignity.

There have been other signals that the leadership of the Orange Order is anxious to avoid confrontation this year, even if its spokesmen have not yet shown the generosity expressed by Fr Scully. Attempts by the grand master, Robert Saulters, to meet the concerns of residents' groups, the fact that senior members of the order travelled to Dublin last week to meet Bertie Ahern, the proposals that have been put forward for a compromise on Drumcree in the *Belfast News Letter* – all these are developments which would not have happened in previous years.

It would be easy to be cynical about this, to point to the dire warnings of the business community and others about the catastrophe of another Drumcree. But equally it is possible to argue that the situation has changed in Northern Ireland in a way that provides some light amid the gloom.

At the political level, these changes are obvious, so much so that we are in danger of taking them for granted. There is a new chief constable of the RUC, Ronnie Flanagan, who is committed to making his force acceptable across the community. The energy and splendid humanity of the secretary of state has the power to kindle hope.

Perhaps she cannot resolve the problems of the marching season, but Mo Mowlam's efforts at least show that someone is in charge who wants to help people to understand each other better and may even persuade them to talk to each other.

But there has been another, more important, level at which change has occurred. The experience of peace, even for 17 months, has had a profound effect on people, shifted their attitudes in a way that could be irreversible. Deep sectarian bitterness remains in sections of both communities, rooted in past suffering and exacerbated by present fears, but there is no appetite for a return to the violence that preceded the 1994 ceasefires.

Peace gave people a glimpse of what life could be like in Northern Ireland and although the mood is fearful and insecure in both communities, nobody wants a return to the days when one dreaded turning on the news in the morning in case six, eight or ten people had been blown to bits. Those 17 months gave them back physical security and the precious, simple pleasures of everyday life.

But peace also gave many people space to think about how the conflict had started and what they might do to ensure that it did not return.

In recent months, I have heard it said again and again by leaders on both sides, those formerly associated with para-military organisations as well as the constitutional parties, that there is no support for a return to conflict. This was one of the main fears expressed at the time by those within the IRA who were opposed to the Hume–Adams initiative, that once the campaign was wound down it would be difficult to crank up renewed support for it.

This is not to say that the IRA is unable to recruit young and committed volunteers. All the evidence suggests that it can still tap these resources. But broad community support for a long terrorist campaign with little prospect of success would be much more difficult.

I was struck last Sunday by how muted the mood was at Sinn Féin's gathering at Bodenstown. The timing, within days of scenes of weeping children at the funerals of the two policemen murdered in Lurgan, underlined the ghastly contradiction between Tone's ideals of uniting Protestant, Catholic and dissenter and the reality of a squalid, divisive conflict in the North.

There have been comments about the marching bands and young girls shouting IRA slogans. My impression was that people felt defensive and fearful about the future. I have been at many similar occasions over the years and Martin McGuinness's speech was notably devoid of the militaristic rhetoric that in the past has sent many a Republican crowd happily home to Belfast. Like Gerry Adams, he knows the community that voted for him in the recent elections does not want a return to the violence and isolation which preceded the IRA'S first ceasefire.

We all know well that the North faces a tense and difficult period. Renewed violence, the political arguments over decommissioning and the run up to the marching season all contribute to a growing pessimism. But even if the news is bleak in the weeks ahead, we should not underestimate how greatly both communities have been changed by peace. It is just possible their resilience and their determination not to let that peace slip away may get us through Drumcree and on to a safer road in the autumn.

Attacks on media must not deter them from doing job

OCTOBER 9, 1997

At the end, nothing became Ray Burke so well as the manner of his going. In his statement on Tuesday afternoon, he gave the importance of the Northern Ireland talks as the main reason for this resignation. "I believe that the holder of my office must be allowed the opportunity of giving total focus to these most pressing issues," he said, explaining that this was impossible for him in the present circumstances.

This measured and direct statement went a good way, at least for this reporter, to justifying his claim that he had always tried "to serve my country to the best of my ability". It put the issue in a proper political perspective and was mercifully free from the mawkish recriminations against his critics which so often figure in these farewells.

It makes it all the more depressing that Bertie Ahern and Fianna Fáil, instead of recognising and matching Mr Burke's dignity, should have reverted to the tedious old rubbish about "the persistent hounding of an honourable man" by the media. It's rubbish because serious questions had been raised about Mr Burke's conduct as a politician and most people would regard it as the legitimate function – duty even – of journalists to try to get answers to them. It is an instinct with most politicians to turn on "the meejia" when they need to draw the wagons around the tribal campfire. Fianna Fáil is no worse than other political parties in this respect. But already it's evident, in telephone calls to radio chat shows and so on, that journalists are once again being accused of driving wholly innocent politicians from public life. It's worth recalling, in the interests of accuracy and a certain professional humility, just how the present spate of scandals came to light.

No journalist was involved in giving large sums of money to a working politician, let alone in setting up offshore bank accounts. The story about Mr Burke came into the public domain because a disaffected employee of the building company involved believed he had been unfairly treated and was determined to tell his story.

It was the same with the revelations about Ben Dunne and his extraordinary gifts to Charles Haughey and others. It is unlikely that we would ever have learnt about the arrangements made to fund the former Taoiseach's lifestyle but for the quarrel between Mr Dunne and his siblings, which is not to detract from the importance of Sam Smyth's original scoop.

There were rumours, of course, in the corridors of Leinster House, particularly about Mr Haughey's wealth. We heard stories about the allocation of government contracts, of huge profits made on conveniently available building sites, of scams on European funds, even of gifts of diamond necklaces and bejewelled daggers. But if there was an accusation to be levelled at the Irish media during what is still loosely called "the Haughey Era", it was how little time and what meagre resources were devoted to probing and investigating these rumours.

A handful of individual journalists proved to be honourable exceptions but, on the whole, far from hounding politicians the media gave them a very easy ride. Let us not forget that even the first of the famous "show tribunals", the inquiry into the beef industry, was set up as the result of a report on Granada TV's *World in Action* programme.

Irish journalists had been accustomed to treating politicians with discretion, rather priding themselves on not reporting on either the financial affairs or the private lives of individual TDs or ministers. In most societies there is a degree of mutual interdependence between journalists and politicians.

Journalists want to keep their sources reasonably happy; politicians want to ensure good coverage of their exploits. But in Ireland, which is a small and gregarious society, this interdependence has been – at least in my experience – much closer than in London, the other place I have worked.

It shouldn't make any difference, but it is in fact much more difficult to write a cold and critical piece about a politician if you know that you are going to meet him or her the next day. I've certainly been guilty of softening reports, or not writing at all about politicians of whom I could have been extremely critical, either because I knew they had a domestic problem or dreaded the phone calls from angry friends attacking me for "picking" on this or that individual.

There were and are more serious reasons which inhibit the vigorous media which we badly need. The libel laws and their application in the courts are the most obvious example. There is the harsh economic reality that investigative journalism of the kind needed to examine meticulously allegations of financial wrongdoing costs a lot of money.

But beyond all this, there was another reason for a certain docility among journalists. Mr Burke touched on it when he said that the rules in 1989, when he accepted £30,000 in cash as a political contribution, were different. The challenge facing not only Bertie Ahern but the whole body politic is to convince us not only that the rules have changed, but that they will be enforced without fear or favour.

That means coming to terms, in a way that has not yet been done, with the legacy of the Haughey era. We should not personalise this unduly, since it is important to our growing political maturity to recognise that the former Taoiseach, however great his present disgrace, did render some service to the State. But it is becoming steadily more evident how far Mr Haughey's code of what was acceptable in politics eroded standards in public life.

Examples are the passports-for-sale affair and the fact that none of the politicians who have been involved in investigating it saw any cause for concern beyond the infringement of "minor" technicalities. Even now, nobody seems prepared to question whether Mr Burke and the Department of Justice could have resisted Mr Haughey's demand that the passports be prepared so that he could hand them over, in the manner of a desert sheikh, to his Arab guests.

Last week, John Bruton said the Taoiseach had told him that he could "finger" up to nine politicians who had received donations as large or larger than the £30,000 which has led to Mr Burke's departure from public life. If this is true, Mr Ahern should tell us how he proposes to deal with these errant politicians. If, on the other hand, the Taoiseach refuses to elaborate further, then we must hope that Irish journalists will pursue the task of discovering what sums of money have been paid to whom and in what circumstances.

As the man said: "News is what someone, somewhere does not want to see published. The rest is advertising."

1998

After being driven mad with grief, long political slog resumes

AUGUST 20, 1998

"I think, as any parent would, of my own sons and daughter. I know I would go mad with grief should it happen to them." The words of Tony Blair, the simplicity of his reaction, go right to the heart of the matter. It was the very ordinary details of the lives so cruelly snuffed out last Saturday in Omagh which brought uncontrollable tears to the eyes and a desire to hug one's own children in wordless gratitude.

The Spanish and Irish kids on a day trip to the wonderful Ulster Folk Park, the young man who had gone into town to spend part of his first week's wages on contact lenses, teenagers working in a charity shop, students waiting for their exam results. It may be that the wave of revulsion will mark a watershed. We have been here so many times before. The statements from the "Real IRA" expressing regret at the casualties and announcing a "suspension" of its activities have been greeted with scepticism by most politicians. But we do know that the anger which followed atrocities like Enniskillen did have an effect in shifting attitudes away from support for the armed struggle and towards politics.

Already the outrage directed against those who planted the

Omagh bomb has been expressed in epithets with which Gerry Adams and Martin McGuinness have long been familiar. "Mindless killers, psychopaths, the dregs of republicanism" – these are words which may help in lancing the immediate pain. But Gerry Adams and Martin McGuinness know very well that the public mood is volatile, that outrage at Omagh will fade, that the argument which underlies this atrocity will not go away.

From the very beginning of the peace process, the first priority for the republican leadership has been to avoid a split. This went beyond an understandable desire to prevent a fratricidal feud. Over and over again, we were told by Sinn Féin leaders that if a split occurred it would mean that those left on the outside would be the most ruthless of the militarists. Understandably, Adams was determined to bring the whole republican movement with him.

It is now clear that a substantial group within the IRA does not believe the peace process is going anywhere. They see the Belfast Agreement as a recipe for disaster, a makeshift solution which is doomed to failure in the long term, leaving the nationalist community in Northern Ireland in a worse state than before.

Many of these people, out of respect for Gerry Adams, have gone along reluctantly with the political process. The difficulties facing the Sinn Féin leadership were seen publicly when the party was forced to reconvene the ard-fheis earlier this year. The appearance of the Balcombe Street gang and other prominent republican prisoners was clearly designed to reassure delegates the IRA was on board. And it seemed that these tactics had carried the day when the ard-fheis voted to support the agreement.

Gerry Adams's reading of broader public opinion within the nationalist community, North and South, was quite correct. What the overwhelming majority of people on both parts of the island want, and what they voted for in the May refer-endum, is the promise of peace and political structures which will allow the constitutional future to look after itself.

But there are still people within the republican movement who see the Belfast Agreement as offering nothing but a reconstituted Stormont, with David Trimble as prime minister and a solid rump of Unionists who are determined to resist any moves towards radical change. As such, they argue, the accord is doomed to fail and will only prolong the agony of sectarian divisions in the North. They see Adams and McGuinness as having been duped, by both governments, into selling out the fundamental principles of republicanism.

I do not pretend to any knowledge of the "Real IRA", but I have been to meetings of the 32-County Sovereignty Movement and I have no doubt that these convictions, albeit mistaken in my view, are passionately and sincerely held. It is all too tempting to dismiss these people as trapped in a time warp dating back to the First Dáil and beyond, but one has only to look at the largely uncritical celebrations of the 1798 bicentenary to wonder whether these views may not be much more widely shared.

This is the problem which faces the two governments as they meet to discuss what security measures should be taken in order to prevent another Omagh. On the one hand, public opinion demands that the bombers be brought to justice. On the other, some of the measures that have been discussed, like internment, could lead to their being regarded as innocent victims within the republican community, with wholly counter-productive results.

It does seem, from talking to sources who know about these things, that the IRA – Real and Provisional – is in a dangerous state of flux, with many of its activists capable of moving forward with Adams into politics, or backwards towards violence.

This poses an even more acute dilemma for the Sinn Féin leadership. At the moment, Gerry Adams and Martin McGuinness are under intense pressure to distance themselves from the "Real IRA", in order to prove that they are now fully paid-up members of the democratic political community. Mr Adams has gone further than ever before in "condemning" the Omagh bomb. But there are increasingly insistent suggestions that the republican leadership should make further gestures of commitment to the peace process, either by decommissioning some weapons, or urging its own supporters to give any information to the security forces.

The immediate reaction that I've had when I've put these suggestions to Sinn Féin members is that any move down this road could: a) put Messrs Adams and McGuinness at physical risk; and, b) precipitate a full-scale, fratricidal republican feud. Everyone in their senses agrees that this would be disastrous. That leaves the other option – the long, hard slog of politics.

It may just be possible that the enormity of public grief and revulsion will work to persuade the various dissident republican groups to abandon violence. But, although it seems almost a cliché to make the point again, the task is to persuade the majority of those, on both sides, who are still tempted in this direction, that politicians working together can bring about change. That is why it is so important that one of the first developments, after the immediate acts of mourning, has been to bring David Trimble to Dublin for talks with Bertie Ahern.

Formula needed to surmount latest peace hurdle

SEPTEMBER 17, 1998

Can General John de Chastelain square the impossible circle on decommissioning? Increasingly the two governments, and political leaders in Northern Ireland who want the Belfast Agreement to work, are looking to this quiet-spoken Canadian to help them surmount the latest hurdle in the peace process.

They hope that he will be able to work out a formula which will persuade reasonable Unionists that the republican movement as a whole is serious about meeting its commitment under the agreement to "the total disarmament of all paramilitary organisations", while at the same time meeting the requirements of the IRA and other groups that such a step should not be construed as surrender.

There is a high level of agreement that General de Chastelain is well qualified for the job. A professional soldier for 40 years, he was taught early to focus his efforts on achieving the main aim of any strategy, which in this case is the securing of the agreement and a stable political settlement. Over the long and frustrating period of the Good Friday negotiations he often acted as George Mitchell's right-hand man and appears, remarkably, to have won the trust of both sides.

He knows that David Trimble and Gerry Adams both want to see this issue resolved so they can get on with the proper business of running Northern Ireland's affairs. But even with this common determination, there are substantial differences between them and serious problems ahead.

The two governments, as well as commentators like myself, have tended to take the rather hopeful view that because so many apparently impossible obstacles have already been overcome, this too will happen with decommissioning. But anyone who has listened to the arguments knows that the issue is a litmus test for each side of the other's commitment to making the Belfast Agreement work.

Over the summer, David Trimble has grown in stature as a leader for the entire community in Northern Ireland, and his opening speech to the Assembly this week underlined this. He is doing his best to leave some room for manoeuvre on the issue of weapons. But he repeats the phrase "Something must be done" like a mantra, and even his closest supporters say that his leadership of the Ulster Unionist Party would be at serious risk if he allowed Sinn Féin to take its seats on an executive before some handover of explosives and arms.

It is perfectly understandable that the broad Unionist community should feel this strongly. There is still a great deal of suspicion on both sides. If Sinn Féin is to demonstrate that it is genuinely committed to peaceful politics, then the IRA must be seen to start the process of decommissioning. Otherwise the fear remains that republicans will return to violence if they do not get their way through democratic methods.

The argument has an added emotional force since Omagh. Sinn Féin may say that the people who made and placed the bomb were nothing to do with them, but there must be concern that in the future, IRA weapons and explosives could find their way into the hands of those dissidents who remain.

Against this, Gerry Adams claims, and David Trimble appears to accept, that the Sinn Féin leadership is not in a position to "deliver" the IRA. Mr Adams argues that the priority must be to implement all the provisions of the Belfast Agreement, seats on the executive as of right for Sinn Féin, North–South bodies, the equality agenda, demilitarisation. When all these things are seen to happen, decommissioning will follow.

The loyalist groups share this view and have made it clear that they will not hand over any weapons in advance of the IRA doing so. They accept the argument that the agreement does not provide for decommissioning as a prerequisite for Sinn Féin taking its seats in an executive and fear that the Unionists will be blamed if there is a serious crisis on the issue.

On the face of it, the two positions are irreconcilable. Sinn Féin may have the text of the agreement on its side, but Unionists can reasonably argue that the spirit of the accord calls for some greater generosity. At the level of realpolitik, there is no point in pushing the issue to the point where David Trimble is isolated from even his loyal supporters or Gerry Adams is no longer able to carry the bulk of the republican movement with him.

It might be that, given sufficient time, the two men could build a basis of trust that would enable them to reach a compromise between them. But that time is not on offer, at least at the moment. Sinn Féin wants seats on the executive to be appointed without delay, to demonstrate to its supporters that there is no pulling back from the agreement. Trimble maintains that this is not possible.

That is why General de Chastelain's strategic skills are so important. We need him to help all sides to find an honourable way out of this impasse. It will help that the goodwill is there. Watching the enormously hopeful scenes at Stormont this week, it has been possible to discern the beginning of what Seamus Mallon describes, with a sense of yearning, as "normal politics".

The exchanges in the chamber have been good-tempered. These men and women treat each other in a way that is remarkably different from the bad old days, when Stormont was characterised by contemptuous arrogance on the Unionist side and impotent anger on the nationalist benches.

David Trimble struck exactly the right note when he spoke of his wish that this should be "a pluralist parliament for a pluralist people", thus acknowledging the changes that have taken place. There is a palpable sense that Sinn Féin and the people it represents have every bit as much right to be there as David Trimble and his colleagues. Together they must share ownership and responsibility for what happens here.

It is already wonderfully easy to imagine Bairbre de Brun answering questions about proposed cuts in education or Reg Empey laying out an environment policy for the north Antrim coast. One of the delegates to Monday's meeting of the Assembly described it as "dull". If that means ordinary and workaday, it's hard to think of a more precious adjective to apply to politics in Northern Ireland. The past 30 years have given us excitement and rivers of tears. We badly need to experience some dullish times.

1999

Sinn Féin must look at the figures that back a political way

MARCH 11, 1999

There is no Plan B. That is the stark and loud message which has come through from both the Taoiseach and the Northern Ireland Secretary, Mo Mowlam. It isn't quite true. If the Belfast Agreement collapses on decommissioning, there will be a return to direct rule with a substantially increased input from the Irish Government. Many of the reforms which are integral to the accord will proceed.

But the real prize – a system of genuine power-sharing government in Belfast and a new relationship between this State and Northern Ireland – will be lost.

The Taoiseach has urged all the parties involved not to "talk up a crisis". Mr Ahern has pointed to the progress that has been made since the agreement was signed less than a year ago.

Even in the euphoria of last Good Friday, it would have been very hard to anticipate that we would see the signing of a formal treaty setting up cross-Border bodies which, if allowed to work, will lead to much closer co-operation between the two parts of the island.

The decommissioning quarrel is a hangover from the past but no less threatening because of that. It could still destroy all that has been achieved. There is a tendency in some quarters to look on both sides with impatience, as though each is being wilfully stubborn.

Why can Unionists not accept that the guns are silent and the IRA ceasefire is for real, particularly since the agreement itself does not require the handover of weapons as a precondition for Sinn Féin taking seats on an executive?

On the other hand, how is it that the republican movement refuses to see that the spirit of the accord demands a gesture to reassure Unionists that the violence is over for good?

Beneath these eminently reasonable arguments there lies the deep mistrust which has always been at the heart of the challenge to find a settlement. The agreement was designed to try to reconcile two opposing visions of the future.

It had to reassure Unionists that Northern Ireland's place within the United Kingdom would no longer be under threat, either from the territorial claim of the Irish Constitution or from IRA violence.

Sinn Féin needed to be able to tell its supporters that the agreement would leave the way open for political methods to achieve a united Ireland, something which violence had signally failed to do.

A number of opinion polls conducted recently in Northern Ireland cast an interesting light on these large issues. A survey carried out by the Institute of Irish Studies at Queen's University found that an overwhelming majority (93 per cent) of people in Northern Ireland want the Belfast Agreement to work.

The overall figure is striking because it must feed through to the political leaders as reflecting a deep and widespread yearning for peace and stability.

But people are more divided as to where the agreement is leading. The opinion poll carried out for the BBC's *Hearts and Minds* programme last week grabbed the headlines because it showed a decline in support for the accord among Unionists. Fifty-five per cent of Unionists voted "Yes" in last May's referendum. If there were to be a rerun today, only 41 per cent would do so.

The response to another question goes a long way to explain their disillusionment. When asked "Do you think Northern Ireland will be part of the United Kingdom in 2020?", 51 per cent of those questioned replied "Yes" and 48 per cent "No".

There has been a steady decrease in the percentage of those who believe Northern Ireland is destined to remain part of the Union, from 61 per cent in 1997 to 51 per cent today. This decline in confidence in the continuing integrity of the UK is particularly striking among Unionists. Just two years ago, 72 per cent of Unionists believed Northern Ireland would continue to remain linked to the rest of the UK. Now that figure is reduced to 61 per cent.

Political leaders are fond of saying opinion polls are only a snapshot of what people think at one moment in time. But these figures must prompt serious assessment in Sinn Féin. They seem to indicate that the Adams/McGuinness strategy of working towards a united Ireland by political means is already yielding results.

Unionists may not like the idea of a break with the UK, but increasingly they accept the likelihood of this happening. This should strengthen Sinn Féin's hand with its own dissidents.

We have been told of the serious danger of a new split among republicans on decommissioning, and even of threats to the life of Gerry Adams. My own impression, after talks with Sinn Féin sources, is that there is a profound mistrust of the whole peace process at grassroots level.

It isn't simply that decommissioning is seen as representing surrender by the IRA. There is also a deep suspicion that, from the very start, the peace process has been a plot engineered by the British government (possibly with Dublin help) to lure Sinn Féin into mainstream politics, thereby weakening the IRA to the point where it is no longer capable of operating an effective armed campaign.

The focus on decommissioning has greatly exacerbated these suspicions, as has the perceived failure by the British – and Irish – governments to "face down" the Unionists on the issue.

I stress that I am simply reporting what has been said to me. I readily concede that this view of what has happened takes no account of the enormous progress which has already been made on many issues, or of the serious difficulties which now face David Trimble. Again, recent opinion polls point these up very starkly.

This is due, at least in part, to the fact that Mr Adams and his colleagues have preferred to concentrate on the perceived bad faith of most of the other parties to the agreement, rather than to highlight the gains Sinn Féin has made, both at a political level and on the equality agenda.

The same accusation can be made, of course, against David Trimble. The Ulster Unionist Party leader rarely recognises publicly that concessions have also been made by the republican movement. But over the past year, the Unionist community has had to accept enormous changes and has done so, on the whole, with a new sense of realism and considerable dignity.

There has been nothing like the protest that one might have expected over, for example, this week's treaty setting up cross-Border bodies. Perhaps it is time for Sinn Féin to recognise how fast the tide is flowing in its direction and to make a suitably generous gesture by way of response.

Referendum essential to decide on Ireland's PfP role

MAY 27, 1999

Riveting as the passing of the *Late Late Show* has been, there have been other programmes on television in recent days. Different, but arguably as important in shaping our understanding of world affairs and Ireland's response to them.

RTÉ deserves our thanks for screening, over three nights this week, *The Death of Yugoslavia*. Made originally for the BBC, this remarkable series takes us back to the political roots of the problems which today face the Western community in Kosovo. It combines the excitement of a tautly plotted thriller with the human grief and devastation which have become so dreadfully familiar on our screens in recent weeks.

The Death of Yugoslavia was made in the wake of the 1995 Dayton Accord, when the participants must have felt free to speak. The programmes include long and extraordinarily frank interviews with all the main players – President Milosevic, the Presidents of Slovenia, Croatia, Bosnia and Montenegro, as well as their top generals, advisers, international diplomats and fixers. The sufferings of ordinary people and the atrocities they endured are not neglected.

The series tells stories of political treachery and

extraordinary heroism – the Serb representative who voted against Belgrade's military intervention in Croatia; the local police chief who went out alone and unarmed, night after night, to try to persuade Serb vigilantes to dismantle roadblocks. He was finally murdered, taking, in his widow's words, "sixteen bullets", of ethnic hatreds and loyalties that crossed all divides.

The series does not make overt judgments, but allows the main participants to speak for themselves. For example, what emerges with terrifying clarity from the second programme is the gross ignorance and complacency with which the political leaders of the European Union dealt with the unfolding tragedy in the Balkans. This included an early attempt to double-cross Milosevic, by bribing Montenegro to vote for secession from the Yugoslav federation – something the Serb leader had already made clear he would not tolerate. But the series is telling, too, on Milosevic's ruthless methods.

A notorious Serb paramilitary leader, responsible for the deaths of several thousand Muslims in the Bosnian town of Zvornik, says, smiling slightly: "Milosevic didn't give us orders – just requests. 'We need your fighters in this town or that.' We didn't let him down."

How does Ireland stand in the present situation? Our forces have played an honourable role as peacekeepers in Bosnia, but we have not distinguished ourselves in our political response to events in Kosovo. "We're between a rock and a hard place on this one," was how David Andrews answered, when asked to comment on the NATO bombings.

Earlier this year, the State signed up to an EU statement which described the NATO intervention as "necessary and warranted", while at the same time insisting that this comment in no way breached our traditional neutrality. This is not only dishonest but politically inept.

We are moving rapidly into a situation where such exercises

in fence-sitting will no longer be possible. We cannot plead ignorance as an excuse this time, as we did for the Holocaust. Programmes like *The Death of Yugoslavia* ensure that we know too much for comfort. And they remind us that members of the European Union have a duty to try to influence that organisation's policies in a way that has not always been the case in the past.

Last week, the Government published *Ireland and the Partnership for Peace: An Explanatory Guide*. This puts the arguments for joining what is described as "a voluntary and co-operative framework for regional security co-operation between NATO and individual non-members of NATO".

In theory, this is meant to be one of the key issues of next month's European elections. The Government has decided that, despite Fianna Fáil's election pledge to hold a referendum, this is not necessary because (in the Taoiseach's words) "a clear democratic mandate will emerge from the European poll".

It is hard to avoid the suspicion that the Government is desperate to avoid a public debate on the issue, because it fears the association in the voters' minds with NATO's debacle in the present conflict and the scenes of misery from the refugee camps in Albania and Macedonia. This betrays, not for the first time, a contempt for the electorate which is quite inappropriate.

There is an appetite for a much broader discussion of what role Ireland should play in shaping and implementing a common security policy in Europe. An opinion poll conducted recently for this newspaper showed that 71 per cent of voters want a referendum on PfP. Last month, a number of public figures, including Bishop Willie Walsh of Killaloe and Seamus Heaney, signed a petition calling for such a poll.

The arguments for and against membership have been well rehearsed in *The Irish Times*. Those against argue that any link with NATO would compromise our traditional policy of neutrality and would ally us to a military organisation over whose decisions we would have no influence. Those in favour of joining PfP point to the membership of other neutral countries, like Austria and Switzerland. Leading members of the Defence Forces say that our failure to join means that our honourable role as a peacekeeping force for the UN has been sidelined to some extent.

It is clear that whatever decision we make about joining Partnership for Peace will be of the utmost importance to the way we see ourselves and to our future role in the European Union. As such, it is important that it be allowed the maximum public debate, rather than leaving the impression that it has somehow been smuggled through in the EU elections.

We are moving towards a European Union very different from the small and homogenous group we joined a quarter of a century ago. Enlargement means that the Union could consist of 25, perhaps even 30, states in the near future. On Monday, Lord Jenkins of Hillhead, a former president of the commission, was in Dublin to give the first Brian Lenihan Memorial Lecture to the Institute of European Affairs.

He spoke extremely warmly of Ireland as a "dependable enthusiast" for greater European integration, and said he believed this was a matter not simply of money, but of political belief. But if we are to fulfil this role with equal enthusiasm in the future, we need to know what it will involve in terms of a common foreign and security policy. A proper public debate demands a referendum. Let the people decide!

Trimble has to convince party it has nothing to fear but fear

OCTOBER 7, 1999

"So, David Trimble has turned out to be a hero?" The question was put to me, with just the faintest hint of irony, by a South African friend in London earlier this week.

This man, who is now in his 70s, spent most of his life fighting apartheid. Much of that time was spent in exile in Europe, though he now lives once again in his own country. I had been asking him how the situation seemed in South Africa. We hear such gloom-filled predictions for the country's future since Nelson Mandela's retirement.

The reports concentrate on the rise in violent crime, a loss of confidence in the Afrikaner community, and the disillusion felt by very many black people that not enough has changed since the first free elections in April 1994.

Did he share this sense of disappointment and these fears? I asked.

"No, no," he cried. "Of course, we face terrible problems. It is a long process changing a whole society. But the country is full of hope. We have escaped the past and there is no going back to it."

I began to feel that I had heard this somewhere before.

Then I realised that it echoed, uncannily, what I had been saying to English friends who had been asking me, in sepulchral tones, if there was any hope for the future of the peace process in Northern Ireland.

So often, because of the nature of the news media, the story told is one of gloom and deep depression. The summer which has just passed is an example.

We have heard much of the threats to peace: the murder of Charles Bennett by the Provisional IRA, the furious reaction of many Unionists to the Patten report on policing, the defection of John Taylor to the anti-agreement camp. And so on.

There has been very little, by comparison, about David Trimble's efforts, in the face of continuing onslaughts from embittered old men and ambitious younger ones, to hold his party together.

I haven't read much about the brilliant poster campaign organised by the Irish Congress of Trades Unions, the Confederation of British Industry and the Northern Ireland Council for Civil Liberties. Under the slogan "Don't be a Chicken – Do the Deal" it urges the political leaders to take courage in their hands.

We know that the situation is particularly difficult just now. George Mitchell, who usually exudes an air of smiling confidence, has told us that the Belfast Agreement could fail.

Such a warning from this source has to be taken seriously, even if its main purpose is to concentrate the minds of all the parties involved as the review process goes into its most crucial week.

First things first. This weekend, David Trimble has, once again, to try to rally his party at the Ulster Unionist conference in Enniskillen. It is likely to be a highly charged gathering at which most issues will be used to attack the Belfast Agreement and, by extension, David Trimble's leadership. Last year's debate on the RUC was dedicated to "our forgotten victims" and the mood on this occasion, post-Patten, is likely to be even more emotional.

The Ulster Unionist leader has made it clear that he intends not only to defend the Belfast Agreement but to lay out in detail why it represents the best hopes for the future of the broad Unionist community. While agreeing that the review process is under stress, Mr Trimble has declared roundly: "I note the eagerness with which some people try to write finis to this operation. I haven't done that yet and I am not thinking in those terms."

This new toughness in Trimble's approach was in evidence last weekend when at a conference of his party's youth wing he spelt out the political realities facing the Unionist community. There was, he said, no possibility of a return to the "immobilism" of the past. Political progress, post-agreement, could only be achieved by creating structures to which all parties, including Sinn Féin, could give their allegiance. If Unionism was seen to destroy the agreement, it would be left totally isolated, shunned by all shades of political opinion in the United Kingdom and, probably, in this State as well.

It was an electrifying speech, provoked in part by James Molyneaux's prophecies of doom made earlier in the day, and deserved much wider coverage than it got in the Irish and British media.

Peace process apparatchiks like myself are perhaps too much inclined to read the runes of other people's success and failure in the area of conflict resolution. Sometimes one can push the comparisons too far.

Forgive me, nonetheless, if I return to the South African experience. Over the summer, I read a powerfully moving account of the proceedings of the Truth and Reconciliation Commission over two years from 1996. *Country of My Skull* is by Antjie Krog, an Afrikaner poet and journalist who covered the hearings of the Commission for the South African Broadcasting Corporation.

It makes for harrowing reading, not only for the testimonies of the witnesses but for the painful honesty of Ms Krog's reactions to them. (It is also a humbling reminder of the scale of other people's problems in the task of laying the past to rest, and the fact that this process has to continue long after the political structures are put in place.)

At one point, the author praises F W de Klerk for his courage in taking the decision to embrace fundamental change in South Africa, but qualifies her tribute by criticising his failure to convince members of his own community that such change was not only necessary, but represented the only possible way forward for them. This omission, she argues, left many Afrikaners bewildered, angry and fearful for the future.

This is exactly the challenge which faces David Trimble this weekend. The evidence of recent weeks, in particular his speech to the young Unionists last weekend, underlines his own intellectual and emotional commitment to making the Belfast Agreement work.

If he can be faulted, it is in that he has failed to convince his own community that the accord offers them their best hope for a peaceful and secure future. His party conference this weekend will provide a platform for him to speak not only to his own members, but to tell the broad Unionist community that there is nothing to fear but fear itself.

PS: In response to the question which started off this column, I replied that, yes, David Trimble had turned out to be a hero, but that the greatest test of his courage will be seen in the coming weeks.

Old allies re-emerge to criticise women who go to work

DECEMBER 9, 1999

A male colleague in this office put one side of the current argument rather well. Charlie McCreevy's Budget, he said, had discriminated against women working in the home "who are performing the most important service to society by rearing stable and secure children".

A number of letters to *The Irish Times* have struck the same note. One correspondent told us that "children only need one thing to achieve happiness and high self-esteem – unconditional love".

OK fellas, we get the drift. Children reared by a mother who works outside the home are less likely to be stable and secure. Their chances of achieving happiness and high self-esteem have been diminished because our decision to take up paid employment – even when economically necessary – has deprived them of "unconditional love".

I've been listening to this kind of stuff for the past 30 years, but my dim eyes can still recognise a reactionary backlash. The comments on Mr McCreevy's moves to individualise the tax rates for married couples have brought the old allies – the Church, Fine Gael and other self-appointed experts – happily back together, expressing views which most of us thought had disappeared from public debate.

Let's get a few facts separated from the rhetoric about the McCreevy Budget. First, nothing in its provisions discriminates against the family in which one breadwinner goes out to work and the other stays at home. On the contrary, couples on a high single income will still do better when costs for childcare and other essentials are taken into account.

Second, in moving towards individualisation, the Budget goes some way to removing the discrimination that has operated against married couples, both of whom work outside the home, for more than 20 years. It doesn't go as far as I (and many other women) would like in recognising that a married woman is an individual who deserves to be treated and taxed in the same way as her unmarried sister. I hadn't intended to write on this issue. For a start, it divides women, and I'm enough of an old-fashioned feminist to dislike that. Of course women have a right to stay at home to rear their children. I welcome Mr McCreevy's move yesterday, which goes some way to recognising the value of their work. But married women also have the right to work outside the home without being penalised for it. That right, believe me, was hard won. I was reluctant to enter the debate precisely because I realise that the statement I've just made will seem like ancient history to many readers. But we forget our history at our peril.

When I got married in the late 1960s, I wasn't allowed to continue working as a journalist. My husband's employers, whom I had never met, simply made this decision for me.

Times and circumstances change. By the time my children were born, I was back at work and the main breadwinner. I worked out of economic necessity. But I also wanted to pursue a job outside the home. It has been an enormous privilege to report on Northern Ireland for the past 30 years. I believe that the media have played an honourable role in exposing discrimination and injustice and I am proud to have been a small part of that.

The life of a working mother is, in some ways, not an easy one. And it's because I now realise that many younger women still have to cope with many of the same pressures that I raise this small voice to protest at much of the comment on Mr McCreevy's Budget. Don't get me wrong. My children, as Cornelia put it, are my jewels. I am constantly humbled and grateful that they are not angrier about the many things of which they were probably deprived. Not unconditional love. That was there but, to use a shorthand phrase, no child in our house ever returned home from school to the reassuring smell of baking bread.

Here are just a few of my memories of trying to balance different sets of responsibilities. There was the constant guilt that the children might be missing out because I was at work. Would they be doing better, feeling more secure if I stayed home? There were attempts to compensate them. I remember driving to Belfast before dawn one Christmas Eve to buy the last-existing "Girl's World" on this island. The toy itself was deeply politically incorrect, being a wax head with false hair that "grew" and accompanying make-up kit. But I have the fondest memories of curling its hair and applying blusher and lipstick to its waxen face.

Alongside this, there was the pressure, more acute in those days I think, not to give any hint to one's employer that one required time off for some family crisis. Most of all, there were the endless nightmares over childcare. One of the reasons I have a high regard for Peter Mandelson, incidentally, is that when we worked together on television programmes, he was endlessly considerate about any crisis which arose over who was minding the children.

Nothing in this column should be taken as approving the broad thrust of Charlie McCreevy's Budget.

I feel deep dismay that he did so little to target social exclusion. On the issue of childcare in particular, there is a need to devote much greater resources (and political commitment) to transforming the situation for all families.

I've been thinking a lot these past few days about Nurse Stoney and how lucky I was to know her. Mrs Stoney ran a local authority crèche in the London borough where we lived when the children were born. We paid nine pence a day for each child and didn't pay anything if, for some reason, the children stayed at home.

For this they were not only fed and cared for, but taken on trips to the seaside, visits to the zoo and had Santa Claus come round on a fire engine for Christmas.

This wonderful place has long since gone. The local council was dominated by "the loony left" and Mrs Thatcher soon put a stop to this kind of tomfoolery. But I still have a photograph of Nursey Stoney, on the beach at Brighton with the children, to remind me of how things could be better for all women who work, inside or outside the home.

2000

A gruesome memorial to a failure to shout "Stop"

June 15, 2000

The battered cardboard suitcases have been placed in neat rows. Some of the smaller ones carry white lettering – KT or Kindertransport – marking them out as having been used by children whose desperate parents begged charitable organisations to take them to England or any other country prepared to accept these small refugees from Hitler's Germany. Most of them never saw their parents again.

It is the mundane details which strike the most powerful chords in the piteous rooms of the Holocaust Exhibition, which has just opened in London. Here are just a few of them: the piles of worn-out shoes, old combs, broken spectacles and toothbrushes taken from inmates of the death camps; hurriedly scribbled notes thrown from the shuttered trains carrying prisoners to Auschwitz, dependent on strangers to stamp and post them to their destinations; a child's school exercise book, in which she has meticulously drawn and coloured every item of the uniform for her school in Birmingham, to send to her parents.

There are also the large and harrowing images of evil: the piles of unburied bodies at Belsen, a scale model of

Auschwitz, demonstrating the extermination process, photographs by SS officers of prisoners throwing themselves against the electrified barbed-wire fences.

Some of these have become almost familiar as ghastly icons of man's inhumanity to man. It is the personal testimony of letters, journals and, crucially, of some 30 survivors who speak from television screens placed throughout the exhibition which give a terrible immediacy to the suffering of millions of individuals.

One man says he spent his whole time in Auschwitz swearing that, if he survived, he would tell the whole world of his experience. It was not so easy. It took 20 years for him to tell anyone and that was only when one of his children said: "Dad, we read such terrible things about the camps. What was it really like?"

One of the exhibits is a clockwork bear, its fur coat rubbed almost threadbare. It belonged to Paul Sondhoff who, as a child in Vienna, was hidden for four years by his elderly piano teacher. The small cupboard was so cramped that his bones became deformed. There were good people who tried to resist what was happening.

One of the most telling photographs shows the smiling doctors and nursing staff at a hospital, one of many, where tens of thousands of disabled patients were assessed for the T4 euthanasia programme.

The exhibition is at the Imperial War Museum, but there is no attempt to draw a veil over Britain's lack of response to the plight of the Jews and other victims: homosexuals, Romany gypsies (wearing the distinctive clothes we see on our city streets) and other outcast groups.

As early as 1939, the British government knew what was going on. Its scientists had broken German codes, but the decision was taken not to publish the information because it would have meant revealing the fact that it was monitoring radio communications.

We are shown the editorials in British newspapers warning against the threat of "an influx of refugees", which could destabilise society at a time when unemployment was running high. It was not until 1944, under pressure from church leaders and others at home, that the allied leaders met to discuss "the refugee problem". By then, five million Jews had been killed.

A recurring theme is the way the whole panoply of law-abiding society in Germany was deployed to create and sustain the image of the Jews as subhuman, abnormal, threatening. The law, schools and universities, artists and the media, factory workers printing the Star of David on great bales of yellow fabric were all drawn in.

It would be inappropriate, perhaps even insulting (albeit unintentionally), to the memory of the millions who died in the Holocaust to draw comparisons between the evil that gripped Europe in the 1930s and 1940s and the challenge which faces us in Ireland today. But I defy any Irish person who visits this exhibition not to feel an uneasy sense of recognition. It is not just the cardboard suitcases and the vile cartoons depicting the Jews as subhuman, the children refused refuge in this State, which stir uncomfortable memories.

We have a Government which seems bent on labelling refugees as alien, different, threatening to our society. Already we refuse to allow them to work, disperse them without warning into fearful and perplexed communities, give them vouchers instead of cash. There are proposals to fingerprint new arrivals and to incarcerate them in flotels. Newspaper headlines warn us of hordes of refugees.

Not surprisingly, perhaps, we see the result of all this in the increasing number of racial attacks on people deemed to be different from us. An English couple, who came to Dublin last weekend to celebrate their wedding anniversary with their son who is working here, were set upon by a group of youths shouting "Niggers out" and wielding knives. Now they have been told not to have "any false hopes" for their father, who is in intensive care in St James's Hospital.

We have a duty – politicians, priests, ordinary citizens – to shout "Stop". It would be a major contribution to that process if this deeply troubling exhibition, which has been four years in the making, could be shown in Ireland.

The Museum of Modern Art at Kilmainham, with its fine lofty rooms, would be an ideal setting. Perhaps Declan McGonagle, the talented and innovative director of the gallery, could propose the idea to Síle de Valera.

Orangemen may lose all marching on

JULY 6, 2000

There is a scene in Gary Mitchell's raw and tender play, *Marching On*, which tells us more about what is happening at Drumcree this week than all the images on television.

It is the eve of the Twelfth of July in a loyalist housing estate in north Belfast. Christopher is a policeman. He was reared by churchgoing, law-abiding parents to accept his responsibilities to his family and the broader Unionist community. That is why he joined the RUC. He has his own fearful memories of violence and keeps his gun close to him at all times.

The war was the easy part. Now he finds himself in a situation where he has to police his own kith and kin on the streets. His elderly father – a decent, God-fearing Orangeman – insists on taking part in a "dignified" protest against the re-routing of the annual parade. His teenage son is, at the very least, flirting with loyalist paramilitaries. The old, familiar world has been turned upside down. And for what? A few yards of road about which nobody outside Northern Ireland gives a toss.

When his play opened at the Lyric Theatre in Belfast last

month, Gary Mitchell wrote in this newspaper about his urgent need to present his own community on the stage. He had listened to so many people in so many pubs, complaining that the Protestant working class had never had a fair hearing, that the media conspired "to make us look like a bunch of unreasonable, irrational, bigoted half-wits".

In a series of passionate and bleakly funny plays, Mitchell has probed the sense of communal defeat, bewilderment and anger that lies behind so much of the violence which we see each night at Drumcree. Like Sean O'Casey's, his characters show us how ordinary people cope – or fail to cope – with the trauma of a civil conflict over which they have no control. The final scene of *Marching On*, where father and son, both in tears, are still unable to communicate with each other, is a desolating picture of loss and loneliness.

Mitchell has written of his community's lack of skills – and perhaps even of interest – in presenting its story to a wider world. This has been very evident in recent days at Drumcree. How could the Orange Order have allowed Johnny Adair and the UFF, the organisation responsible for some of the most vicious attacks on innocent Catholics, within a hundred miles of Drumcree?

Their presence, together with that of the LVF, might have been designed to alienate sympathy in the broader Unionist community, which deeply resents seeing the adjective, Protestant, linked to this kind of thing.

The television images of Drumcree, however shocking, must not stop the rest of us from trying to understand the deeper emotions that underlie the protest. The hardline Orange leader who compared the loyalist community to a "wounded lion" was probably a bit over the top, but he was close to the mark when he said that many of the ordinary, working-class Protestants at Portadown felt "abandoned".

David Trimble and a large section of middle-class unionism

have accepted that the old days have gone forever. The Unionist hegemony has been broken into small pieces. They have looked at the figures and know that time is on the side of the nationalist community. An internal research document drawn up for the UUP traces the decline in the Unionist vote and argues that Unionists could be in a minority in the Assembly within 10 years. "In fact, we may be grateful for mandatory power-sharing," the author comments tersely.

Against this background, David Trimble and his colleagues negotiated the best possible deal to protect the interests of the Unionist community. In the Belfast Agreement, Irish nationalism agreed to the principle of majority consent in order to achieve a political settlement. As important, the republican movement recognised that it was crucial to have peace and stability so that the two communities could learn to work together and to trust one another. Nothing of lasting value would be gained by achieving a united Ireland in which a large section of the Protestant minority would continue to be as alienated from the new order as Catholics had been from the old.

This is the reality which loyalists and Orangemen at Drumcree have yet to understand and accept. It may be that their own leaders have not done enough to explain it to them. But this week's attempt by the DUP and other anti-agreement Unionists to expel Sinn Féin from the executive showed very clearly that there is no going back. David Trimble described the DUP motion as "irresponsible" and bound to heighten tensions at Drumcree. Changed times indeed!

Trimble's comment also highlights another reality of this whole process, which is that any act of generosity by one side helps to settle the other in a way which improves the prospects for both communities. The IRA's recent statement on the inspection of arms dumps is the most obvious recent example of this. By making what was for the whole republican movement a difficult and brave decision, the IRA has bolstered David Trimble's confidence in a dramatic fashion and enabled the UUP leader to be brave in his turn.

To return for a moment to Drumcree. The scenes of violence which seem set to continue for the next week will repel Irish nationalists, just as they shame and embarrass very many Unionists. But it is not so very long since images of nationalist violence filled our screens and were universally condemned as the actions of brain-dead thugs. We need a more sympathetic understanding of what lies behind the ugly scenes at Drumcree. It would help, I believe, if the Abbey Theatre, which has staged Gary Mitchell's plays in the past, could bring *Marching On* to Dublin.

2001

The anger we must not ignore

Glen Branagh will be buried in north Belfast today, a day short of his 17th birthday. He died in horrific circumstances on Sunday night when the pipe bomb he was carrying exploded. Eyewitnesses said his hand and part of his arm was severed from his body and that he received head injuries, from which he later died in hospital.

After the high hopes and emotions which have attended the restoration of political institutions in Northern Ireland, the story of Glen Branagh, who died defending Protestant Ulster, is a terrible reminder of the realities that underlie the whole peace process.

The circumstances of his death are already the stuff of bitterly contested myths. The police who were on duty in north Belfast on Sunday night say a masked man came running out of the Protestant crowd "carrying a fizzing object in his hand and was moving to throw it at our lines when it exploded, killing him".

Loyalist leaders in the area claim the bomb was thrown by republicans from the Catholic side and that Branagh was trying to get rid of it. Eddie McClean, a Protestant community worker in the area, said: "He died a hero's death, trying to save other people." Gerry Kelly of Sinn Féin hotly denies this version of events and has said he is certain the bomb was not thrown by nationalists.

At a small shrine marking the place where the teenager died, there are UDA flags, a Rangers' supporter's scarf, red poppies and a wreath from the Ulster Young Militants, the youth wing of the UDA of which Branagh was a member.

The riots on Sunday night, the worst sectarian clashes which Belfast has seen during the current phase of the peace process, were sparked off – God help us all – by a Remembrance Day service in North Queen Street. Loyalists say nationalists living in the area attempted to disrupt the ceremony. Nationalists reply that they have been under siege all summer and were terrified when they saw loyalist youths break away from the main Protestant group.

By nightfall, the scene was set for a confrontation which cost one Catholic man the sight of an eye, led to a 12-year-old Protestant boy having to have twenty-eight stitches in his neck, and resulted in twenty-four policemen and two British soldiers being injured.

Glen Branagh's death has been described as "the senseless waste of a young life" by David Trimble and as "an appalling waste which demonstrates that sectarian violence brings nothing but pain to communities that have suffered too much already" by the NIO minister, Jane Kennedy.

Alban Maginnis of the SDLP has called for legislation covering sectarian "hate crime" to deal with the kind of events we have been seeing in north Belfast. All of these reactions are understandable. What they do not begin to address is the key question – why was a 16-year-old Protestant living in north Belfast so consumed with anger that he was prepared to risk his life in order to hurl a bomb at his neighbours, who happened to be Catholic, or at the police who were, as he saw it, preventing him from doing this?

We know, or think we know, some of the answers. This

area has long been an ugly cockpit of sectarian tensions, where one community or the other constantly feels under threat. As Billy Hutchinson remarked, we know the hatred exists; the question is how to change the situation. Some years ago, I interviewed the actor, Kenneth Branagh, about his childhood in north Belfast. His family lived in Mountcollyer Street, just beside Mountcollyer Avenue where Glen Branagh's parents now reside. (No, I have not been able to establish whether their families are related.) The actor who, to his credit, has never forgotten his Belfast roots, was extremely warm about his early years in a mixed street where children ran in and out of each other's houses without a bother on them.

Then came August 1969. Within a matter of days, trucks and lorries arrived in Mountcollyer Street. Overnight, or so it seemed to him as a child, the Catholic families disappeared. Soon afterwards, his father moved his young family to England.

Glen Branagh was not so fortunate. It is not enough to say about his death that it was senseless or that he was being manipulated by evil men. I am old enough to remember when such comments were made about Catholic teenagers who were involved in the IRA. Many of these former young people are now members of the Assembly and have played a valuable part in the search for peace.

A way has to be found to bring the community which Glen Branagh was attempting to defend into the process, to deal with their fears and grievances through political dialogue. Last weekend, at the SDLP conference, Mark Durkan told his audience that he had been invited to speak to the North Down branch of the UUP. That is a move, from both sides, which is both brave and genuinely welcome. But, as we all know, there are not likely to be many teenagers, Catholic or

Protestant, wanting to throw bombs at their neighbours in north Down.

Today, Glen Branagh will probably be given a martyr's funeral, just as the IRA man, Thomas Begley, was after he died placing a bomb in a fish-and-chip shop on the Shankill Road.

The challenge which faces the political class in Northern Ireland now – and by that I mean church leaders, the business community, the trades unions, community groups as well as politicians – is to create a society where no teenager places his or her hopes for the future in making or carrying a bomb.

Observer *was willing to look at North*

DECEMBER 13, 2001

"Idon't know why you keep going back there. It's never going to be a big story." It was early in 1969 and I had been asked to come along to the *Sunday Times* to discuss joining the paper. The senior executive who was interviewing me was talking about Northern Ireland, way back in those innocent days when the civil rights movement was in its infancy, before the arrival of the British troops or the birth of the Provisional IRA.

"My editor thinks it's a story," I said humbly, lacking the courage to walk out of the room there and then. I was working at the time as a reporter on the *Observer*. I had been sent to Derry in the autumn of 1968 and had been deeply shocked by what I saw there. Back at the *Observer*, where the great and the good discussed apartheid, the precise state of the Cold War, and human rights abuses across the world, nobody had ever heard of Northern Ireland. It simply didn't figure in the British media.

At the Wednesday morning editorial conference, I started to talk about what I had seen in Derry – the desperate poverty, the discrimination, the hopeless feeling that nothing would ever change. Above all, there was the fact that these things happened to people because they were Catholics.

David Astor (a former editor of the *Observer* who died last week) cut me short. "Go away and write it," he said. "Write as much as you need. It's our job to find the space." The article was carried in the newspaper on October 6th, 1968, the day after the first civil rights march in Derry was beaten off the streets by the RUC. The paper carried it on the front page beside a picture of Gerry Fitt, at that time a Westminster MP, with blood streaming from his head. It caused quite a stir.

Much more important, though, was that Astor kept sending me back, week after week, to Northern Ireland. Often, there was little to report. The civil rights marches were determinedly non-violent and respectable, led by men and women who believed that political and social justice could be achieved by these methods. There was little interest in the British press. But Astor persisted in running front-page stories, backed by editorials pleading with the British government to introduce substantial reforms before the situation exploded.

He got little thanks for his pains. I learnt afterwards that he came under considerable pressure from the British government to give up the reports from Northern Ireland because they were causing serious embarrassment abroad.

This was a distance from the way I had joined the paper some years before. I had been working as a feature writer at *Vogue*, and Astor had read an interview I'd done with Philip Larkin. I was invited to join the paper as fashion editor. I knew little about fashion apart from what I'd absorbed at *Vogue* by watching people like David Bailey and Jean Shrimpton, but I jumped at the offer.

The *Observer* under Astor's editorship was already legendary. His famous editorial excoriating the British government's attack on Suez in 1956 lost the paper many readers and even more advertising revenue, but became a flag for campaigning journalism. Orwell had written for the *Observer*. So had Isaiah Berlin, Arthur Koestler and other political giants.

Amnesty International grew out of an article in the newspaper. It campaigned against apartheid and for a settlement which would give justice to the Palestinians in the Middle East. Among people who wrote for the paper while I was there were Patrick O'Donovan, Neal Ascherson, Philip Toynbee, Kenneth Tynan, Mark Frankland and Michael Frayn.

As it turned out, my ignorance of fashion wasn't a handicap since the *Observer* didn't really approve of such frivolity anyway. I found the job extremely difficult, and my task wasn't made easier by the fact that my early pieces had to be read not only by the editor but by the science correspondent. I solved the problem by treating the subject as a mix of theatre and social history which pleased my colleagues but not the advertisers.

One of Astor's great qualities as an editor was that he didn't put his journalists in boxes. One day, when I was struggling with an article on the hidden significance of the miniskirt, I got a call from the arts editor.

"Ken is going away for a few weeks. The editor wants you to fill in." My stunned silence left the obvious question hanging in the air.

"I don't know why," he continued in a puzzled tone. "He says he thinks you'd be a fresh voice."

Going to Northern Ireland was almost as fortuitous. By that time, I was writing a weekly column, another idea of Astor's, which looked at the problems which ordinary people experienced with the institutions of the state.

I'd written to Gerry Fitt, who turned up at the newspaper with a battered suitcase full of newspaper clippings. Before I knew what was happening, he had whisked me off to meet Austin Currie and then on to Derry.

I must have been a sore trial to Astor at that time because my reports from Northern Ireland were both emotional and partisan. But gradually he and other people at the *Observer* taught me to be a journalist. What I learnt there shaped the political and social values which have guided me ever since.

One of the most important lessons which Astor taught me is that an independent, liberal and crusading newspaper is crucial to the health of a democratic society. It is a thought which has been much in my mind in recent weeks as we, at *The Irish Times*, have faced our own crises.

2002

Resignations set important precedent

APRIL 11, 2002

If a week is a long time in politics, a month can seem more like a century in the working life of a journalist. After five weeks' reluctant absence from this privileged space, I return to find an altered state. How else can one describe the news of not one, but two resignations by powerful men from public life?

This is not written in any spirit of gloating. On the contrary, the decisions of Bishop Brendan Comiskey two weeks ago, and of Bobby Molloy yesterday, should be welcomed, with some gratitude, by the citizens of both parts of Ireland. Whatever the individual motives that prompted each man to act – and obviously these were a mix of political and personal pressures – the end result is the same.

A prince of the church and a senior politician have accepted responsibility publicly for their mistakes and admitted that their failures are such as to leave them no course but to give up their jobs. In a society where it is almost unheard of for public figures to accept blame, let alone resign, for their past actions, this must (surely?) have an impact on the way that church and state conduct their affairs.

The resignations appear to have taken the media and the

general public by surprise. The full story of Bobby Molloy's attempts to contact a high court judge, on behalf of the defendant's relative, in an appalling case of incestuous rape, is still unfolding. But one has only to contrast the former minister's swift and dignified statement yesterday morning with the shuffling and prevarication of Ray Burke, Hugh O'Flaherty, Michael Lowry, etc., to understand the public amazement.

By contrast, the fact that both Mary Harney and Bertie Ahern had already moved to support Mr Molloy and express the view that his actions did not amount to a resigning matter came as no surprise at all. For many people it simply underlined how far the Tánaiste, despite her repeated calls for probity in public life, has fallen into line with traditional Fianna Fáil thinking on such issues.

Ms Harney was at it again yesterday in an article in this newspaper stressing the Progressive Democrats' commitment to the path of incorruptible virtue. "My vision for Ireland is for the content of our character, not just for things. I want high standards to be our starting point, our very heart and soul, our shared values," she wrote. How ironic that it should be left to Bobby Molloy, by departing from politics and from the PDs, to indicate how those words might be given practical effect.

The case of Bishop Brendan Comiskey is rather different. His failure to deal with the case of Fr Sean Fortune has caused enormous, perhaps irreparable, suffering to many innocent people. The facts have been known for a long time. My colleague, Alison O'Connor, chronicled the whole sorry story in her fine book, *A Message from Heaven.* The BBC documentary, in which a number of Fr Fortune's victims were given space to speak of their experiences, gave wider publicity to these facts.

Brendan Comiskey is not the first nor the last Irish bishop to have failed grossly in his duty to protect innocent children in cases of sexual and physical abuse. As the televised excerpts of the Hierarchy's press conference at Maynooth earlier this week demonstrated all too clearly, the instinct to safeguard the institution, if necessary by protecting the abuser, still runs very deep.

Over the years, Dr Comiskey has struck many of us, not exactly wholehearted admirers of the Catholic hierarchy, as a humane man who has struggled to open a wider debate within the church on issues such as clerical celibacy. He is also the first Irish bishop to accept publicly that his failure to deal with the problem of child sex abuse in his own diocese renders him unfit for his holy office.

His resignation has played an important part in forcing the Irish hierarchy, some of them very reluctantly, to face up to the enormity of their responsibility for what has happened to so many Irish children over the years.

I don't want to appear starry-eyed over these events. We have yet to see whether these resignations, welcome though they may be, will have a lasting impact. Both Bobby Molloy and Brendan Comiskey had their own reasons for the decisions which they made.

Mr Molloy, after 37 years in the Dáil, had not achieved the kind of status he probably felt he deserved. As a loyal member of the Progressive Democrats, he was often ignored in favour of more starry performers such as Michael McDowell. He had already indicated that he was reluctant to fight another general election. He must have known that this story would run and run particularly if, as now seems likely, there is more grime in the pot.

In Bishop Comiskey's case, there were even stronger reasons for throwing in the towel. Whatever the nature of the Government's proposed inquiry into clerical abuse in the diocese of Ferns, it is going to be a difficult and extremely painful experience for everybody involved. Already there are arguments over how far the bishops will be prepared to co-operate, given the Vatican's sensitivities on the issue worldwide.

Whatever the motives that prompted Mr Molloy and Bishop Comiskey to act as they did, their resignations set an important precedent in Irish public life. It will not be quite so easy in future for men and women in powerful positions to shuffle off responsibility for their own failures and misjudgments. But this will happen only if we, the public, insist that they are held to account. It is an opportunity which we must not waste.

Give thanks for how far we have travelled

APRIL 18, 2002

Is it possible to imagine a day when Yasser Arafat is able to host a dinner in an elegant hotel in Jerusalem at which the chairman of the Palestinian Authority pays tribute to the courage and idealism of the suicide bombers who have brought death and a legacy of grief to so many Israeli families?

Almost as important, will Mr Arafat ever feel able to tell the people of Jenin and Ramallah that it is time to recognise that both sides have endured terrible suffering during the long years of conflict in the Middle East and to hold out a hand of reconciliation to old enemies as well as friends?

The idea sounds far-fetched and will certainly be offensive to many people whose hearts go out to those Israeli families who have lost children on the streets of Haifa and Tel Aviv.

The more detached observer, horrified by the toll of death and destruction seen each night on the TV news, knows that such an occasion is something devoutly to be wished.

The US Secretary of State, Colin Powell, for example, must surely recognise that the rituals of ending a bitter conflict are a necessary part of the healing process, and infinitely preferable to the continuation of war.

Gerry Adams has been attacked for his speech last weekend at a dinner held in Dublin to honour the IRA's dead. Politicians on both sides of the Border – and of the sectarian divide – have described it as a glorification of violence.

Michael McDowell has pointed to the contradiction between the Sinn Féin leader's readiness to flaunt his party's links with the IRA, while at the same time refusing to give evidence to committees of the Dáil and the US Congress on what he knows about the Colombia episode.

In *The Irish Times,* my colleague, Kevin Myers, asks why a blind eye is consistently turned to crimes which police on both sides of the Border believe to have been committed by the Provisional IRA.

One answer, which seems to me to be worthy of serious consideration, is that history takes a very long time to lay to rest.

Like many people, I first dared to hope that peace might be possible in Northern Ireland back in September 1993, when Yitzhak Rabin shook hands with Yasser Arafat on the lawn outside the White House. I remember watching television, with the tears pouring down my cheeks, as the whole world waited for the eternity it seemed to take for Bill Clinton gently to urge the Israeli prime minister forward.

When Rabin spoke, his words were directed to the people living on the West Bank: "We who have come from a land where parents bury their children, who have fought against you, the Palestinians, say to you today, in a loud and clear voice, enough of bloodshed and tears. Enough."

That was a year before the first IRA ceasefire, at a time when parents still wept at funerals in Belfast and Derry.

How fortunate we have been and how much we owe to the vision and determination of political leaders in both parts of this island.

Our own peace process has been rocky and is still

considerably fraught with problems. Brutal criminal acts are still committed by paramilitaries on both sides, including the Provisional IRA. As Gerry Adams himself said: "It hasn't gone away, you know."

But at least, and we should be grateful for it, the IRA is on a relatively tight leash.

Those of its members who remain opposed to the Belfast Agreement and see every move in the peace process as a sell-out have been, to a large extent, sidelined.

Because the republican movement is obsessively secretive, we get only very rare glimpses of how difficult and dangerous this process has been for Gerry Adams and his colleagues.

The Colombia adventure is the most obvious example of this. Michael McDowell has accused the Sinn Féin leader of having "a yellow streak" (what a deliciously old-fashioned term of abuse!) for his refusal to give evidence about the episode to an Oireachtas committee and to the US Congress.

There are other points to consider. Adams and those close to him appear to have been taken by surprise by the presence of the three men in Colombia and of their relationship with FARC. If this is the case, the events constitute the most serious challenge to Adams's authority, and to his credibility within the republican movement, since the Good Friday agreement was signed in 1998.

The peace is not perfect, far from it. We are still a long way from the hopes expressed by both Gerry Adams and Martin McGuinness that the IRA should go into voluntary retirement. Already, I can sense outraged readers writing in to complain that this column is "soft" on murdering gangsters. Before you reach for your pen, consider what might have been.

Look at the video of the grave young Palestinian woman as she explains why she is about to blow herself to bits.

Give thanks for how far we have travelled

Listen to the Israeli parents who weep for the innocent teenagers who became her victims.

Then give thanks to whatever God you worship for how far we have travelled and beg Her to help Yasser Arafat and Ariel Sharon to find the same road.

What is the stars?
That is the question

MAY 30, 2002

Once upon a time and in another country, I saw Nureyev dance *Le Corsaire*. More than 30 years later, I still close my eyes and recall that performance – the Russian dancer's soaring grace, the awesome control of his body, his passionate intensity. It was the closest I have ever come to seeing the presence of the divine made manifest in a human being.

I don't remember any of the details surrounding the performance: who accompanied me to Covent Garden, what we did before or afterwards. I think I knew, because it was common gossip, that Nureyev was "impossible", that he threw tantrums and made excessive demands of other dancers and of the theatres where he chose to perform.

None of that mattered, then or now. What impelled a usually rather reticent London audience to its feet for a standing ovation, to look at each other with something close to terror, was the knowledge that we had just seen something miraculous on stage and that, as spectators, we were part of it.

Let's not push the comparison too far. Nobody, as far as I remember, ever suggested that Nureyev had a responsibility to

253

act as a role model for young people or that the hopes of an entire nation were riding on those flying feet.

That is a new phenomenon which athletes like Roy Keane and David Beckham seem to accept, perhaps unwisely, as part of what goes with being a superstar. But watching Keane's interview with Tommie Gorman, I was struck by the fact that, as with Nureyev, words were irrelevant. Keane's body language told us what we needed to know.

I have been privileged in my working life to report on great historic events in this island. I know well that peace in Northern Ireland (which was not, incidentally, achieved by political leaders of uniformly sunny disposition) is far more important than any football tournament or stage production. Yet the memories which sustain my belief in the human spirit are not of the announcement that a deal had been struck on the terms of the Belfast Agreement, or of Margaret Thatcher and Garret FitzGerald signing the Anglo-Irish Treaty in 1985. They are of great performances by those whom we rightly call stars because they shed light upon our lives for years to come and in ways that we cannot fully comprehend.

Because my own trade is words, these experiences have been mainly in the theatre – Paul Scofield in *King Lear*, Donal McCann in *The Faith Healer*, Fiona Shaw as Electra. For others, this necessary contact with something beyond the material world is channelled through religion or arts other than drama.

For many millions, it comes through sport, particularly football which cuts across creed, class and colour. We know that in Ireland, besides giving pleasure to many fans, it has helped us through times when questions of national pride and patriotism have been problematic, to put it mildly.

The vast majority of us cannot begin fully to understand what courage it takes for an actor or athlete to put him or herself on the public stage, hoping each day or night to achieve perfection, vulnerable to the slightest mishap.

Over the years, without any particular psychological skills, I've interviewed or talked to a considerable number of these sacred monsters. However great my admiration for the individual's gifts, the process has rarely been easy. More often than not, he or she has struck me as driven, obsessional, almost wholly self-absorbed and, to use the current jargon, quite pitifully "needy".

I remember a truly great English actor telling me how much he dreaded returning from holiday and opening his mail. This was before the days of mobile phones and instant electronic communications. If there were no scripts for him to read or other demands for his talents, he became immediately convinced that he had been forgotten, wiped from the affections of his peers and his public. I thought of him when Roy Keane told Tommie Gorman how hurt he felt, sitting alone in his room, that so few of his team-mates or members of the FAI had tried to talk to him after the bust-up with Mick McCarthy.

Whole forests have been pulped in the attempt to explain what the row between Keane and his manager means to us in Ireland and abroad. I am well aware that I am not qualified to enter that debate, though I have questions I would like to put to the man himself.

The only point I am trying to make here is that we common mortals owe a debt that we can never fully repay to those whom the gods have chosen as performing artists – actors, musicians, athletes. It is they who give us the stuff of dreams in our youth and memories in our declining years. We should value them accordingly.

So, given that we are all seeking "closure", what should we do on Saturday? I will watch the Irish team and will cheer them on in good company. My thoughts will be with our lost captain. In the evening, I plan to go to the Gate Theatre in

Dublin. There is a new play on by Frank McGuinness which I want to see anyway. But the main reason for my visit will be a personal act of gratitude to Alan Howard, the actor who has the role of Mícheál MacLiammóir.

He played Oberon in Peter Brook's legendary production of *A Midsummer Night's Dream.* No one who saw that will forget him reclining on a trapeze above the stage, then swinging out towards the audience while his glorious voice transported us to Shakespeare's world of magic, human foolishness and lovers reconciled.